RV Living for Beginners

The Complete Guide for Discovering How to Live your Full-Time RV Life Off-Grid and Enjoying Rving Lifestyle: Camping, Boondocking, Van Dwelling by Travelling. Even with family

Table of Contents

Chapter 1: RV Living
Chapter 2: The Right RV
Chapter 3: The RV Systems and Maintenance
Chapter 4: The RV Life
Chapter 5: Full-Time Rv-ing with Family
Chapter 6: Boondocking

Chapter 1: RV Living

What is Full-Time RV Living?

Full-time Being a "full-timer" or RVing simply means spending all of your nights in your RV. It's your house, your one and only home, and it's all I have. It has nothing to do with age, wealth, or where you come from to be a full-timer. In fact, camping and RVing are more popular in other countries than they are in the United States.

People who want to travel and explore the globe full-time are known as full-timers. They seek complete independence from financial obligations such as mortgages, physical obligations such as foundations, and social obligations such as keeping up with the Joneses.

When you work full-time, you have the following options:

- Not being bound by mortgages, debts, or the monotony of a single location
- You are free to live wherever you desire. (In our experience, this has included beachfronts along the Pacific Ocean, riverfronts, lakefronts, mountaintops, on a volcano, farms, wineries, national forests, and even New York City!)
- Work from anywhere
- Meet new people
- Spend more time in nature
- Save a ton of money
- Basically, do anything you want all the time

All of this might be summed up in a single sentence: The best option is to go full-time.

Why is RV-Living Becoming More Popular?

The world has altered in a million different ways during the last several decades. But there's one way that's the most overwhelming: we have more options than any culture has ever had. Do you have a supermarket store that doesn't have great avocados? There are probably five others within walking distance of your home. You're not a fan of Shell petrol stations? There are a slew of different possibilities available to you. Is there nothing decent on TV? Don't worry, there are millions of television series and films available on cable, satellite, and the Internet. You don't want to be confined to an office? You can work from home, a co-working place, Starbucks, a wifi-enabled bar, or a coast-side RV (yes, I've done all of these). Every day, we are presented with more options than we know what to do with. One of them is living in an RV and traveling full-time. Despite this, everyone lives in a house with four walls and running water. Most individuals I know live in what we RVers refer to as a "sticks-and-bricks" or "brick-and-mortar" home. This is excellent news whether you're concerned about tornadoes or want a steady, predictable future. However, it is not ideal if you want to explore the world, learn and grow, and become a better person (all of these are side effects of full-time travel). So you could sit around like everyone else and whine about property taxes and traffic and how annoying HOAs are and how you don't understand why everyone cares about the Kardashians because you don't care about the Kardashians, but you'll still wind up talking about the Kardashians no matter what. Or, you can try full timing. When we first started our RV adventures, there weren't many resources for full-timers. We disregarded prudence and learnt as we went. In retrospect, it seems a little crazy and risky, but it's better than daydreaming about the future.

Pros of RV Living

If you're thinking about acquiring a motorhome or simply want to avoid having to reserve a hotel room, or simply want to avoid the expenditures of air, land, and sea travel, you should be aware of the benefits as well as the drawbacks — first, the benefits. Having an RV allows you to be mobile. You already have everything it takes to be continuously on the move if you own an RV. You can leave today for Ridgewood and arrive in New York City tomorrow. After that, you can go to Las Vegas the next day. You can go to as many places as your RV can take you.
As long as you have gas and your car is in good working order. The RV windshield is large enough for you to take in the scenery as you go. Its purpose is to allow you to view every aspect of where you are and where you're heading. If you're driving with your kids, they'll love the view because everything is presented on a transparent glass plate.

With an RV, you can see locations, take pictures with your camera if you want, and visit important sites or landmarks to create lasting memories. Being higher up off the road surface in your RV makes movement much more delightful, because there will be times when you will feel as if you are floating. Some folks have taken hundreds of fantastic windshield photos and assembled a gallery of them. While you may get a similar experience in an SUV, the panoramic perspective provided by an RV is just incomparable. You not only have the freedom to move when and how you like, but you also get to enjoy the side attractions. The beautiful surroundings are completely yours to enjoy. The sight-seeing is really breathtaking.

If you want to experience the Great Smoky Mountains, Rocky Mountains, Yosemite, or Yellowstone National Parks without paying for a field trip or a grand tour, the RV life is for you. This broadens your geographic knowledge and allows you to write a book on it. With an RV, you can visit areas you've always wanted to visit. There will be no more delusions, only reality. What's more, you'll be able to bring all of your stuff as well as your family with you. A road van is indeed that large and accommodating. Clothing, food, accessories, hardware, utensils, literature, and everything else you may think of can all be stored in an RV. Oh, and don't forget about the pets!

- Inexpensiveness

If you're thinking about acquiring a motorhome or simply want to avoid having to reserve a hotel room, or simply want to avoid the expenditures of air, land, and sea travel, you need be aware of both the advantages and disadvantages – first, the advantages.

You are mobile if you own an RV. You already have everything it takes to be on the move all of the time if you have an RV. Today you can be in Ridgewood, and tomorrow you can be in New York City. The next day, go to Las Vegas. You can go wherever your RV can go.

As long as you've got gas and your car is in decent working order. The RV windshield is large enough to allow you to take in the scenery as you go. It is intended to allow you to view every aspect of where you are and where you intend to go. If you're driving with your children, they'll be enthralled with the scenery, which will be shown on a plate of transparent glass.

With an RV, you can see locations, photograph them if you like, and visit important sites or landmarks to create memories. Being higher off the ground in your RV makes mobility even more delightful, because there will be times when you will feel as if you are hovering. Some people have taken hundreds of outstanding windshield photographs and assembled a collection. While an SUV can provide a similar view, the panoramic vista provided by an RV is just incomparable. You not only have the freedom to travel when and how you like, but you also have the opportunity to take in the side attractions. You have complete access to the lovely surroundings. The sights to see are breathtaking.

If you want to see the Great Smoky Mountains, Rocky Mountains, Yosemite, or Yellowstone National Parks without having to pay for a field trip or a grand tour, the RV life is for you. This broadens your geographic knowledge and allows you to write a book on the subject. You can visit areas you've always wanted to visit with an RV. There will be no more fantasies, only reality from now on. Even better, you can bring your entire family and belongings with you. Yes, a road van is that spacious. Clothing, food, accessories, hardware, utensils, literature, and just about everything else you can think of may all be stored in an RV. And don't forget about the animals!

- Home away from Home, yet Comfortable

When I was a kid, I heard that there is no place like home. Wasn't it something like the Wizard of Oz? When they say "home," they don't always mean four walls and a one-hundred-dollar roof over your head with some out-of-this-world chandelier dangling from it. Not really.

Home can be found wherever the heart is. It's even possible that it's a tree. No, I'm not talking about the monkey tree. I'm referring to the treehouse. My point is that while you're driving down the highways and back roads in your RV, you're not in your house with all the sofas and ergonomic chairs, but you're still in a home, somewhere you can feel comfortable and relax. It usually entails having your own bedroom, bathroom, and, of course, restroom.

Your kitchen is also with you at all times. Some road vans are large enough to accommodate all of these features and more. If you have the cravings halfway over the Rocky Mountains, pull over to make some popcorn, smoothies, or eat a snack until you're satisfied, take a toilet break, and get back on the road! If you're stuck between cities and it's late, and you're worried about driving late in the dark, you can park near a truck stop or parking lot and spend the night for about $5.

If the prospect of bed bugs sucking the life out of you gives you the creeps, you can sleep in the comfort of your own bed instead of lugging your luggage into a hotel room. You may appreciate nature while still eating pizza by stopping by a lake and taking in the view while also taking advantage of the conveniences of the great indoors. For some of us, the best part is having a toilet nearby anytime we need it, whether for pee breaks or when our children become car sick. There's no need to pay to use a restroom or go into the woods to relieve yourself.

Everything has been designed to ensure and improve comfort. If that is ever going to happen, having my wife cook while I fish by the Amazon has to be the pinnacle of any of my RV excursions. Because the heart may be anywhere, your heart can be with your RV.

- You Become Part of the Community

I'm referring to the RV driver and lifestyle traveler communities. This is more than just a matter of Facebook fan sites and Twitter trends. If you are the type of traveler who stops at RV campgrounds and makes overnight reservations, there is a good possibility you will meet new people and make new friends, the majority of whom will be RV travelers just like you.

When was the last time you truly got to know your hotel neighbors, and, dare I ask, when was the last time you really got to know your hotel neighbors? The majority of folks simply check in and out without saying hello to the person next door. I believe the only time you knock on that door is to complain about the decibels disrupting your sleep and to request that the loud neighbor tone down the level of the rock or electric music! But why not say hello while you're at it?

One of the benefits of being an RV traveler is that you get to socialize more than the average person. And if that pesky neighbor starts to irritate you, you can take a bow while the applause is still going strong. There was no intention of making a joke. Is there any at all? So, you get the idea. It becomes so much pleasure to meet others who share your thoughts and lifestyle when you become a member of that travelers' community. And if you chance to meet someone as wonderful and thrilling who is traveling in the same direction as you, you team up and give the road a run for its money! If you're curious, RV owners and travelers treat one another like brothers and sisters in the same industry, similar to how fellow Harley Davidson owners treat one another — you're still different people who happen to share a common bond miraculously, and as a result, you treat and address one another with respect, share your passions, and discuss your goals.

Is there anything more intriguing on the road than meeting new people? People have met, married, and started families as a result of such road meetings, and they are still on the move! All of these things can happen in a conventional hotel or restaurant, but in my experience, they are significantly less common. Simplicity Have you ever felt like your life is too complicated? Are you bothered by the idea that the things you have to consider and deal with are too complicated for you to handle?

Have you ever wished for a simpler life, where you knew exactly what you were doing and how to go about it? One of the better possibilities is to live in an RV. Yes! Simple! With the RV lifestyle, you'll be able to eliminate a lot of unnecessary expenses, such as having friends over for the weekend and spending a lot of money to entertain them. That is not something that everyone can afford. If being in two places at the same time sounds like too much of a nutjob, your best bet for making everything one-plus-one is to acquire an RV and travel away from quantum physics. At that luncheon affair, you won't need to wear a tuxedo to impress anyone.

I've even seen and heard of RV drivers traveling with nothing on but their underwear. It may be that hot at times, and the RV lifestyle is all about freedom. You can live and exist in a single enclosure without becoming bored. You think it's dull? Wait until you're driving through the Appalachians or on a safari and a full-grown elephant chases the smoke out your back.

You have the freedom to live your life at your own speed. You get to get rid of everything that causes you stress and drains the light from your pockets, wallet, and bank account. You will be able to put money aside for the future. You become a more natural person if you live in an RV. Because you're around by a lot of people who notice how others appear, talk, and act, you don't get to make up who you are. You get to be no one but yourself in your own road van and in your own comfort. You get to be yourself while also having fun. There are no strings connected. You lead a simple existence!

Cons of RV Living

- Expensiveness

I know I mentioned affordability as one of the benefits. And now we have an additional cost to consider. Oh, come on, it's not entirely free of charge. Is that what you expected? Nah. To purchase an RV, you will, of course, require funds. Depending on your final decision, purchasing this vehicle will almost certainly have a financial impact. You're essentially buying a moving house, so you should be prepared to foot the expense. You'll also require funds for gas.
You'll be on the road for the most of the day. While having a gas-efficient RV is a great idea, you'll still need to plan for how you'll fill up that tank. Then there are the supplies. You will need food for your journey because you will not be able to afford to dine out in restaurants or standard eateries. The larger the company, the more materials are available. If you're traveling with your entire nuclear family, you'll need to consider their stomachs as well. Hunger is the worst thing that can happen to you while RVing.
There is no enjoyment when you are hungry. There isn't one. As a result, you and your companions must eat healthily. It requires money to buy canned meals, drinks, beverages, snacks, and other delicacies from a nearby supermarket and stack them in the RV. A lot of it appeals to me. And as time goes on, all of these resources will run out, and you will need to replace them when you arrive at new locations. Not to worry; compared to living in a house and owning a car, this is still a cheaper way to live.

- Storage and space

You won't be able to bring all of your belongings with you, no matter how big your RV is. Yes, these vehicles exist in a variety of shapes and sizes, but there is a limit to how enormous they can get. Your 24-inch HDTV and deep freezer from your previous apartment will not fit. You'll have to sell or give away your California King Bed.

You won't be able to take bubble baths in a large bathtub because this type of bathroom will be less comfortable than the ones you used to eat in. You cannot bring all of your possessions on board, especially if you are traveling with your family; just the most critical ones are permitted.

Have you seen that massive electric cooker? You can't even begin to consider it. Put it on the market. Because your RV will come with many things on a smaller scale, putting the gaudy items into the vehicle would be pointless due to the restricted space. Don't be like the Indians and Pakistanis, who travel with a plethora of cargo piled high atop their trucks. Get in the habit of traveling light. Your life will become more simpler and you will begin to spend less if you learn to survive with only a few items. It makes sense.

Now, just so this doesn't come across as more of a pro than a drawback, traveling in an RV necessitates extreme self-control when it comes to the amount of luggage you bring. You can't carry everything and anything at the same time. Your mind is playing tricks on you by persuading you to bring the mini-fridge with you, but where will you store it? What's hidden behind the driver's seat? You will, in fact, need to utilize the refrigerator provided by the RV.

- Unfamiliarity

The more you REV your way from one location to the next, the less familiar you become with local service providers. You realize it will take some time to adjust to a new environment or community with each step you take. You will be unfamiliar with service providers such as mechanics, internet or reception, haircut salons, notary public, dental clinics, and all-around medical facilities, and thus will not know which is the best to patronize.

You'll also meet odd people, some of whom will be hesitant to assist you right away because you're a stranger to them as well. And, as we were taught as children, don't talk to strangers. Haha..! You may also lose track of your whereabouts if you do not have a GPS tracking device or if it becomes malfunctioning, or if the map becomes too complex or difficult for you to grasp. You may be mugged or robbed as a result of this. Or you could get lost, putting everything in jeopardy.

- Breakages and Minor Mishaps

If you choose to live in an RV full-time, you will be on the road for every day of the month and every month of the year. As a result, if you drive frequently, items will begin to wear, tear, and eventually break. Unknowingly, a child from a new neighbor may throw a rock at your windshield.

While trying to navigate a tiny passage, you may collide with another vehicle. RVs are motorhomes that are subjected to the effects and abuse of highways and roadways at speeds of 60+ mph in more ways than one. And it just so happens that many of the systems installed in some RVs are of dubious quality to begin with. So, if we do the arithmetic and you've traveled 50, 000 miles in ten years, things will begin to fall in a predictable pattern and, eventually, break off. Most of them, at least.

It could happen inside or outside the RV. If you are not a handyman when it comes to these minor fixes, your vehicle may not be completely safe. When you consider traffic and the few service providers you may encounter, you may find yourself abandoning the RV lifestyle sooner than you expect.

Chapter 2: The Right RV

Different types of RV

Most people who are new to RVing have no idea what types of RVs are available or what size would be ideal for them. I'll go over the different sorts of RVs briefly here so you know what you have to work with when it comes time to rent one before buying one.

- Truck Campers: These are small in size and make it easy to get around the neighborhood to and from your camping. This is popular with customers since it can be attached to a pickup truck's chassis or bed. It will allow you to travel to more remote regions and is ideal for family recreational camping.
- Class A RV: This is the largest motorhome class available. It can grow to be as large as 30 feet in length. Although they resemble a bus, they do not require any specific training or permits to operate. The main benefit of this RV category is its spaciousness. It's ideal for families who require more space to move about. The biggest downside is that they are more difficult to run and are frequently too large to enter certain campgrounds or remote areas.
- Class B RV: The size of this RV is smaller than that of a Class A or Class C. It can be anything from 18 to 24 feet long. These are popular among folks who don't want to drive a big car or tow a trailer around. The key benefits are that they are less difficult to maneuver and navigate than larger versions. The biggest downside is that they are less spacious, making traveling with your family unpleasant.
- Class C RV's: The size of this RV is usually less than that of a Class A. It has a length of 18 to 29 feet. The primary benefit of this class is that it includes cabover beds, which provide additional sleeping space. The main disadvantage is that it is less spacious than a Class A and more complicated to operate than a Class B.
- 5th Wheel Trailer: 5th wheel trailers are basically two-story pickup truck RVs. One level sits in the bed of your vehicle, while the other follows behind it. These typically sleep two to six persons. It all depends on the model you have and how your floor plan is laid out. Towing a 5th wheel is more convenient and stable than towing a travel trailer. A travel trailer has less space than a fifth wheel trailer. This allows you to take more luxurious stuff with you on the road.

- Travel Trailers: These trailers are made to be towed by a van, automobile, or pickup truck with the help of a frame hitch or bumper. A travel trailer offers all of the conveniences of home and is ideal for all types of RV lifestyle. A travel trailer's key advantages are that it may be hauled by lighter vehicles and that it is simple to unhitch. A travel trailer's main disadvantages are that they are more difficult to tow and more unsafe than 5th wheel trailers.

Most Important Factors to Consider When Choosing an RV

Having the appropriate features in your RV can make or break your trip. You want to make sure you have everything you need to survive and thrive while traveling. You don't have to rough it when you live in an RV. You can live a simple lifestyle if you wish, but you can also have all of the conveniences of home while on the road. When purchasing an RV, there are a few crucial features to consider.

- Space: If having extra space on the road is important to you, an RV with higher ceilings, more leg room, and deeper cabinets might be right for you. Just keep in mind that the more room you have, the more expensive it will become. A larger RV will also be more difficult to maneuver and manoeuvre than a smaller RV. You should be aware that certain RV parks and highways have size restrictions, so keep that in mind.
- Connectivity: Do you desire Internet access for both business and pleasure? Do you want to put a satellite dish on your television? Do you want a home theater system, an LCD television, satellite radio, or iPod and MP3 connectivity? A Powerline energy management system is something to think about if you want a lot of these high-tech toys. It will help to reduce the amount of electricity used by your RV.
- Earth Friendly: Do you want to be able to run your devices on solar power, have energy-efficient appliances, or even use wind turbines to power them? Paying for some of these features may be something you want to consider if you place a priority on environmentally friendly solutions.

- Safety: For many of us with family, safety in our RV is a top consideration. If you share this sentiment, you might want to consider RVs that have a sturdy chassis and are more resistant to the elements and rust. You should also check to see if your RV has air bags, circuit breakers, and electronic monitoring systems that can monitor things like tire pressure and vehicle stability.
- Driver Convenience: When travelling across the country, you want the experience to be as smooth and comfortable as possible. Making sure I had GPS, rear vision cameras, reclining bucket seats, and emergency start assistance switches was one of the areas I concentrated on throughout my RV search.
- Floor Plans and Furniture: Because this will be your home, having a footprint that is suitable for you and your family is essential. Is it vital to have high-end finishes and high-quality furniture? Do you prefer more or fewer cooking appliances in your kitchen? How many beds will you require? All of these are questions you should consider before making a purchase.
- Slide Outs: These are extensions that pull out of the side of your RV to provide you more space, as the name implies. Extra bedroom space, extra kitchen space, and extra living room space are all instances of slide outs. Some things to keep in mind about slide outs is that they can break down mechanically over time, resulting in leaks and electrical concerns. Slide outs provide a lot of conveniences and more room, but they also come with the risk of future maintenance; it's all a matter of priorities for you as a buyer.
- Fuel Efficiency: RVs are known for guzzling a lot of gas. Manufacturers have begun to include additional fuel efficiency measures in recent years, which you should examine. You can choose between a standard RV and a hybrid model RV, which can obtain up to 40% higher fuel mileage. You can also choose an RV that is less in weight and has a good aerodynamic front profile for better fuel efficiency.

Thing You Must Know Before You Buy a Used RV

Finding a good used RV can be like looking for a needle in a haystack at times. When you're out shopping, keep the following in mind:

- Does the person showing you the RV actually own it?

First and foremost, double-check that your contact is the RV's owner. The father of the man who owned the rig showed us the first-class C motorhome we looked at. He didn't know the answers to our questions, and he had no control over the RV's price. He couldn't tell us how it was stored (which was crucial), how often it was driven, or show us any maintenance records. Make sure you can ask the owner questions directly, unless the owner is deceased or you're buying from a used RV dealer.

- How many people have owned this RV, and how often have they driven it?

Franklin was our fourth ownership. He was purchased new by an older man, then owned by a younger man for less than two years, and then utilized by a family of four for regular camping vacations. After the family relocated from California to Texas, we bought the rig from them.
This is how we knew it was a positive sign:
The truck had made it all the way from California to Texas and was still going strong. Because the owners had children, they would be extra cautious in maintaining a vehicle they could trust to transport their children. We didn't know much about the previous owners' use of the RV, but we knew it was kept up and utilized on a regular basis at least recently.
Note: Reduced mileage isn't always a desirable thing when purchasing a used RV. When someone drives an RV frequently, it's usually a sign that it's in good shape. If you buy a used RV with little miles, it could have been sitting on an empty lot for a long time, and you could end up with a lot of problems.

- Do they have maintenance records?

When it comes to purchasing a used RV, maintenance records are the holy grail. We were told right away that the transmission had been changed in 2012 and that the RV's cab had suffered leak damage and had been completely redone. Every prior RV owner has meticulously recorded all of the RV's maintenance documents. This demonstrated that they were responsible enough to rectify the problem (as well as retain the records) and offered us peace of mind that everything was well.

- How many miles are on the tires and when were they last replaced?

You should be able to figure this out quite quickly if you collect maintenance data from the prior owner. If you're seeking to buy a used Class A RV, this is very vital. Tires on Class A rigs are incredibly expensive, and replacing them is comparable to paying for college. Last summer, we observed that our front two tires were wearing unevenly owing to a manufacturing alignment issue and needed to be replaced right away. Thankfully, everything was covered under warranty, as the cost came to a stunning $300 per tire. Ugh. Examine the tires thoroughly! Checking the tread is simple even if you don't know much about tires. Do they appear to be faded and sun-damaged? If that's the case, they're definitely nearing the end of their lives. Do some research on how much it would cost to replace all of the necessary tires, and then request a discount on the RV's price.

- Check Everywhere for water damage.

Examine the roof and the area around all windows. Feel for spongy spots on the walls that could suggest prior or ongoing water damage. Water damage is, in my opinion, the most important reason to avoid purchasing a secondhand RV. If an RV has been damaged by water, save your money and don't buy it. What is the explanation for this? It's often difficult to determine the extent of the water damage until you start digging into the wall. One small soft spot could cause a lot more damage than you think. We discovered a soft place in the bottom left corner of a window, back behind the dining room chair, after purchasing our RV. Because the chair continually blocked this region, it was impossible to see, but after a large downpour in Nebraska, we observed a small puddle of water on the floor. This leak became a continual source of frustration for us and a valuable lesson in RV sealing. (We strongly advise all RVers to travel with Eternabond tape, the gods' sealant.)

- Press all the buttons.

Start the engine (when applicable). Turn on all of the lights. Outside, look for clearance and brake lights. Start the generator (when applicable). Make sure the jacks are level. Warm up the water by turning on the hot water heater. Take a look at the water pump. All of the faucets should be turned on. Every feature should be tested to ensure that it works. The last thing you want to discover while boondocking one weekend is that your water pump has failed.

- Stand in the shower.

This is something I'm serious about. I only showered in Franklin when it was absolutely necessary. The shower was far too small for a relaxing experience. In addition, my first shower experience was less than ideal, and I vowed to avoid showering in the future. (Don't worry, I was still clean because I used RV park showers!) Whether you're tall, try standing in the shower to see if you can manage it. While it may seem insignificant today, trust me when I say you'll be grateful to have a rig with a good shower after three months on the road.

- Check under the unit for damage, rust, etc.

We (mainly Heath, ahem) scraped our back end on so many steep driveways on Franklin that the metal wheels that keep your back end from dragging were busted. When we sold our RV, the wheels were nothing more than semi-circles. While not a deal-breaker for the buyer, pay attention to the RV's underbelly and how it's been maintained. Look for rust, cracks, and clearly broken wheels, among other things.

- Ask what animals have lived in the RV and for how long.

Because Heath is allergic to cats, this is a must-have for us. You can typically tell by odors, but it's crucial to ask if you have any allergies. Inquire about smokers as well.

- Ask for a test drive.

Most owners will allow you take a test drive in their vehicle. If they don't, don't purchase it. A major red flag has been raised. Take the rig out on the open road (especially if it's your first time driving an RV!) and have some fun. Examine how the rig reacts to varied speeds, turning, stopping, swerving, and other maneuvers. Do this on a windy day to get a true sense of the RV's sway. How are you getting along behind the wheel? Is it really too huge for you, or do you think you'll be able to acclimatize to it? Take the rig up a couple hills and listen to the engine if you plan on visiting a national park with mountains (specific to motorhomes). Is it excessively hot, or does it complain about the incline? Keep in mind that the rig you're testing is probably empty, and it'll be substantially heavier when it's loaded with your possessions, family, and full tanks. Listen for objects that are rattling and moving when the rig is moving (or have whoever is looking at the rig with you listen). This isn't a deal-breaker, but it can be aggravating. I know a couple who bought a Thor and had an entire cabinet fall out of the ceiling and smash to the ground while traveling. As a result, paying attention to these noises is crucial!

- Ask for an inspection.

It's well worth the money–probably less than $200. Before you buy, ask the owner whether you can have the rig properly inspected. We didn't buy a truck camper since we asked for one and were flatly refused. If the owner isn't concealing anything, they'll most likely agree. This is primarily for your own peace of mind when purchasing a secondhand RV. I'd say you're ready to start bargaining on the price if your setup passes the third-party inspection!

- Can you extend the warranty?

You may be able to purchase an extended RV warranty for your used RV, depending on the model. I can get you an estimate for extended coverage through a firm called Wholesale Warranties. This would be an extra fee, but it could be a smart alternative for peace of mind and, in the long run, saving you money on costly repairs. If you buy from a dealership, you may be able to get a warranty as well.

Chapter 3: The RV Systems and Maintenance

RV Water System

What Is an RV Water System?

Water intake, storage, filtration, heating, and disposal are all part of your RV's water system. Does it appear to be difficult? The entire system may be divided into three sections: how you receive your water (fresh water intake), how you utilize your water (plumbing system), and what you do with your waste water once you're done (your storage and dumping system.)

RV Freshwater System Explained

Given the significant variations between your RV's water system and your home's water system, let's go over the most significant distinctions.

- City Water

Hooking up your RV to what is known as "city water" is the easiest way to achieve a similar experience to your at-home water. Whether you're utilizing a campground hookup or a household faucet, all pressured external water sources are referred to as this. Your rig will have a city water port somewhere on the outside where you may connect your hose.
Use a hose meant for drinking water, not just any old garden hose. To avoid potential significant damage to your rig from overly pressurized water, place a water pressure regulator between your municipal water source and your RV water system.
Using city water eliminates the need for your RV's fresh water tank and allows you to get water directly from your faucets and other fixtures. This method is only available in RV parks, campgrounds, residences, or other locations where you can tap into a stable pressurized water source.

- Freshwater Holding Tank

You'll use your RV's fresh water holding tank for the rest of the period. These come in a variety of sizes, but most will last at least a few days of dry camping or "boondocking" before needing to be refilled.
Fill your tanks with as much water as you'll need for the trip before heading out to camp at a place without water. Keep in mind how much more water will add to the total weight of your setup. It's also crucial to clean and sanitize this tank once or twice a year.

- Water Pump

You'll need to utilize your water pump to transport the water from your holding tank to your fixtures if you don't have access to city water.

This pump is usually controlled by a switch positioned among the other controls for your RV's systems. In some circumstances, you'll be able to turn on the pump and it will turn on when it's needed. In other cases, you'll have to manually switch it on and off.

- Water Filters

For their RV water system, the majority of RVers will utilize at least one filter. This makes sense, as regular travelers may be unsure about the quality of their water supply.

These filters are frequently seen on the rig's outside, where the city water supply enters the water system. They are available in a variety of filtering techniques, including sediment-based, carbon-based, and ceramic.

These filters are essential for removing unpleasant flavors, smells, and pollutants. They also keep small particles out of your RV's water system and pump, which might cause them to malfunction. Additional filters can be installed on your faucet, or jug-style filters, like as Brita pitchers, can be used.

- RV Water Heater

What good is a shower or basin in an RV if the water isn't hot? That's when the water heater in your trailer comes in handy. Your rig's water heater is probably likewise controlled by a switch. Water heaters in RVs can be propane, electric, or a combination of both.

However, don't expect hot showers as you would at home. Water heaters in RVs are sometimes chastised for not being able to produce enough hot water for long showers. That's not unexpected, given the average volume of 10 gallons or less.

Tankless RV water heaters try to alleviate this problem by heating water throughout your RV's water system. These, on the other hand, are usually more expensive and, in some situations, more difficult to maintain.

RV Water System Plumbing Explained

Let's take a look at how your water gets from your RV hookup to all of your water-based systems.

- Kitchen

Your sink is the focal point of your kitchen's water system. The water in your sink comes from either your fresh water tank or a city water supply. As previously indicated, many RVers will either install a filter in their sink or re-filter their sink water in a Brita or other portable filter.

Grey water is the water that runs down the kitchen sink. Food scraps, detergent, and anything else that runs down your sink have contaminated this water. Drain screens are recommended to keep anything too large from getting down there.

- Bathroom

The water system in your bathroom is divided into two parts: one for the shower and one for the toilet. Both use the same fresh water supply, whether it's from your tank or from city water. Your shower, like your kitchen sink, emits grey water that is full of debris, body oil, soaps, and shampoos.
Your toilet, on the other hand, produces "black water," which is water tainted with human waste and toilet paper. To avoid clogged tanks in RV water systems, you must use specific toilet paper.

- Grey Tank

Your grey water is stored in the grey tank. Even while grey water isn't quite as bad as raw sewage, you should still be careful where and how you discard it. This water is filthy, yet it's nothing compared to...

- Black Tank

...in your black tank's black water. As previously said, this is where you'll locate your rig's human waste and sewage. How and where you can dump your blank tank are governed by tight rules and regulations. To avoid accumulation, black tanks must be cleaned and deodorized on a regular basis with particular cleansers and deodorizers.

RV Waste Water and Dumping

Okay, you've used up all of your water. So, what's next? While you're camping, your tanks will be able to hold this effluent. It's time to dump your tanks when you've filled them or concluded your trip. Dump stations are provided at most RV parks and campgrounds, while some can be found at highway rest areas or specific outdoor commercial chains.
You should wear rubber gloves for this because you will be touching raw sewage. Connect your RV's tank valve to the dump station with a sewage connection, then dump away. Empty your black tank first, then your grey tank, in that order. This allows you to rinse the remnants of your black water out of your hoses with your grey water. After dumping, it's also a good idea to rinse your sewer hose with fresh water.
Enjoy Your Water!
As you can see, your RV water system has a few additional considerations than your house water system. But if you follow these rules, you'll be enjoying hot showers and pleasant drinking water in no time - and with fewer toilet water problems!

Cleaning RV Water System

Cleaning and disinfecting the tanks is perhaps the most crucial element of your RV water system maintenance routine. Cleaning out the wastewater tanks is vital for getting an accurate reading on your water level meters, and here's how to accomplish it.

We'll focus on how to clean your RV's fresh water tank in this section because it's one of the most important aspects of the system. You may notice a foul odor or taste in the fresh water coming through your faucets if you let your tank run too long without a sanitation treatment. Fortunately, disinfecting your RV's potable water tank couldn't be easier - which is all the more reason you should do it on a regular basis. All you'll need is a little bleach from around the house!

Here's how to do it.

1. Any water in your freshwater holding tanks should be totally drained.

If you have a hot water tank, keep in mind that it may need to be drained separately. However, don't try to drain it when it's hot or under pressure, as this could cause injury! To avoid damage to the system, turn on the water pump to drive any remaining water out. Turn it off as soon as the water stops draining.

2. Make the bleach solution.

We'll use a simple mixture of bleach and fresh water to clean your water tank. In a one-gallon bucket, mix a quarter cup of bleach with standard tap water for every 15 gallons of fresh water tank capacity in your RV. If you have a 45-gallon fresh water tank, for example, you would simply pour 3/4 cup bleach into the bucket and top it over with municipal water. It's true that a little goes a long way!

3. Fill the tanks with the bleach mixture and add it to your water system.

After that, you'll need to add bleach to the water system. This is a simple step: just pour the mixture into the tank! Always use caution when putting pure bleach into your RV's fresh water tank. Because bleach is so potent, it could cause harm.

4. Ascertain that the bleach solution has completely treated the tank and plumbing lines.

After you've placed the mixture into the tank, continue to fill it with regular, fresh water until it's full. Turn on your water pump and run all of your interior taps, including your shower, until you smell bleach in the water after it has been filled. This guarantees that the inbound pipes are sanitized as well.

Turn off the faucets and the water pump, and leave the bleach solution in your water tank for at least 12 hours. Driving around to assist distribute the mixture evenly along the holding tank walls may also be beneficial.

5. Remove the bleached water.

Drain the tank thoroughly to get rid of the sanitation liquid once you've given it time to clean and disinfect it.

6. Fresh water should be added to the tanks.

After that, add a fresh batch of clean water to your tank, completely filling it.

7. Drain the remaining water, and your tanks are now clean and ready to use!

Drain the second batch of water, making sure the drainage liquid no longer smells like bleach. You may need to repeat this step a few times to guarantee that all of the bleach has been removed from the system — which is critical because you'll be utilizing this tank to store water that you'll drink soon!

After you've double-checked that the bleach is completely gone, your tank is ready to be filled with drinkable water for your next camping trip!

RV Solar Power System

To different people, a "RV system" (small boat and cabin systems are nearly identical) can mean different things. It may be as simple as a 5-watt panel that keeps the battery charged in between journeys or over the winter. It can entail 900 watts of solar panel (or as much as will fit), a huge battery bank, and an inverter for someone who lives in one full time. Almost all solar panels are water and salt spray resistant, and all but the smallest come with a 20 to 25-year warranty. We've sold a couple to RVers who like to park for a while. Wind generators are common on yachts and for rural residences.

The majority of RV and boat lighting and accessories are powered by 12 volts DC. Solar panels and batteries can easily power all of these. Switching to DC fluorescents, such as the "Thin-Lite" 12-Volt fluorescent lights, can minimize your power requirements and the number of solar panels required. These lights emit the same amount of light as incandescents while drawing less than one-third the electricity.

Depending on how much power you use, the number of panels and battery capacity you need. If all you need are lights, a small TV, and the typical built-in gizmos, 80 to 130 watts of panels and a strong heavy-duty deep-cycle battery should suffice. If you want to use an inverter to power a microwave, coffee maker, vacuum cleaner, or other conventional AC appliances, you'll need a larger solar panel, usually around 200 to 400 watts.

Although 12-volt DC fluorescent lights and a few other 12-volt appliances, such as ceiling fans, are available, 12-volt appliances are often of lower quality and cost far more than normal household appliances. Most RVs contain an inverter, which can range in size from a 250-watt unit for occasional use to a 4000-watt pure sine wave one with a built-in battery charger.

Batteries

How much battery:

Battery requirements vary greatly, but for all but small RVs and trailer campers, 200 to 225 amp-hour capacity is considered the minimum. Aside from that, it's usually a matter of space and a place to store any spare batteries. While you may "require" 800 amp-hours of capacity, if you just have half that, you'll have to be more careful with your power consumption.

Two 6-volt batteries in series (golf cart size) are neither better or more reliable than a single huge 12-volt or two 12-volt batteries in parallel, contrary to popular perception. Because 6-volt golf cart batteries were the only generally accessible deep cycle batteries at the time, there was some truth to the rumor. It's crucial not to combine old and fresh batteries in a set, or different types (particularly gelled) with other types, regardless of the arrangement or size you use. If the age gap between old and new batteries is more than a year, it could cause problems - and more than three years is usually a clear "bad thing." Most RV house battery systems should have a battery storage capacity of 200 to 600 amp-hours or more.

Gel-Cells: Some people have had success with gelled cells, but our results have been mixed. Gel-cell batteries will not withstand the same amount of abuse as flooded or AGM batteries. One issue with gelled cells is that they are significantly more susceptible to overcharging damage. Gelled batteries are no longer available.

You'll almost certainly need an inverter. To prevent significant connection costs and voltage dips, large inverters should be placed as close to the battery bank as possible. You may estimate how much battery you'll need (in amp-hours) by calculating how many watts you'll require every day and assuming that your batteries can provide at least twice that (you don't want to run your batteries completely dead). To calculate watts, multiply volts by amps; for example, a 12-volt lamp that draws 3 amps consumes 36 watts, and a 12-volt battery capable of 100 AH consumes 12 x 100, or 1200 watts (however, if you pull the full 1200, your battery will be dead, so figure at least a 50 percent safety factor or 600 watts). Visit our battery page for a lot more information on batteries. The 36-watt light would run for nearly 20 hours on the same battery.

Inverters

Small inverters are inexpensive and capable of handling light loads; for instance, a 75-watt inverter can power small notebook PCs. A microwave inverter (800-1200 watts) or coffee maker inverter could cost $500-$1100. The larger sine-wave inverters, which can produce 1000-4000 watts, will cost anywhere between $1000 and $2600. Inverters in the 800-to-2500-watt range are sufficient for most RVs and boats, with 1000 to 1500 watts being the most common. A comprehensive system, including the panels, batteries, inverter, and other components required for full-time living, might cost anywhere from $1800 to $5000. Because not enough panels and/or batteries can be put in the limited space, that size system may not be practical for some RVs and boats. A system with 150 to 300 watts of panel, four to eight 6-Volt deep cycle batteries, a charge controller, and an 800-to-1500-watt inverter is the most common size. Visit our inverter page for further information and specifications. Between the battery and the inverter, there should always be a fuse or breaker - this is commonly a "class T," JJN, or R type fuse (DC breakers are pretty expensive).

Hybrid Systems

Solar + Generator: A "hybrid" system is used by many people. They use solar for minor loads that are required on a regular basis, such as lights. They can power TVs, PCs, and most other small gadgets with a tiny 250–800 watt inverter. For the heavy loads, they use a generator. It may seem unusual to have both, but the solar system eliminates the need to operate the generator all of the time only to power modest loads, charge batteries, or power short-term heavy loads like a microwave. Running a generator full-time can be costly, and it can irritate your neighbors. You might use the generator for an hour or two a week with a hybrid setup. In many hybrid systems, the generator can also be used to charge the solar system batteries via the inverter if there are a few overcast days. If the RV or boat is not utilized for long periods of time, the solar panels ensure that the batteries remain fully charged. A wind generator and solar panels can be included in a hybrid system, which is very useful for boats. As a general rule, 130 watts will reduce the demand for a generator charger by 60 to 80 percent.

Converters

A battery charger is referred to as a converter. Most factory-installed converters charge the batteries at around the same rate as 1 to 2 panels (3 to 10 amps), and have poor regulation and charge characteristics (there are a few exceptions - some Magnetek RVs now come with competent chargers). Many emit an excessively high voltage after the batteries have been charged, and if left on continually, will damage the batteries. Some battery manufacturers refuse to provide warranties for batteries that have been charged with a converter.

If your batteries are worth more than a few dollars, ditch the converter and rely on solar panels and/or an inverter with a good 3-stage charger, or invest in a well-regulated charger like the Iota charger. A step-down transformer and a rectifier are the only components of a small converter. Because of their low power, recharging a big battery bank might take hours or even days; recharging a single 200 AH battery bank from a tiny converter could take 30-50 hours.

Mounts

We recommend the flat or "flush" mount for most RV systems. Tilting mounts are available and will improve your power by roughly 10% to 20% in optimal conditions. Unless you're planning to be in one location for a long time, most people find that the hassle of getting up on the roof and placing the mounts, as well as making sure the RV is always positioned so the panels can face due south, is more trouble than it's worth. When traveling, the tilting mounts cannot be left up. Almost every tilting mount will tilt left or right.

It is ideal to mount any panel with a very tiny tilt, no more than 5%, so that standing water does not accumulate on the panel and any rain washes away the dust.

The following is a typical medium-use RV or cabin system:

- 1 or 2 80 to 150-watt solar modules, such as the [Solartech SPM085](#) or [Kyocera KD150.](#)

- 1 - panel mounts for roof mounting.

- 1 - Morningstar solar charge controller

- 4 - 220 amp-hour 6-Volt deep cycle batteries (golf-cart size), or 2 Concorde 4D's

- 1 - 600 to 1500 watt inverter.

- A modest "beginning" system can cost as little as $400, and a big system with a sine wave inverter can cost as much as $4,000 or more. The typical cost is roughly $900, but this varies greatly.

This system's total daily energy output is around 1600 watt-hours, which should be enough to run most basic RV lights and appliances, as well as small AC appliances. Depending on the specific components utilized, the cost could range from $1800 to $2300. Single-panel starter systems can be had for as little as $400. A simple starter system might consist of only a single panel, mount, and charge controller.

Economics and Lifestyle Factors

Before purchasing an RV system, there are two things to consider: is it worth it, and why is it worth it?
The cost of the system is the most obvious consideration; solar is not cheap, and it may not be suitable for everyone. It will save you money on generator fuel, wear, and maintenance, but not enough to be profitable. Other factors to consider include the fact that solar is very quiet and requires very little maintenance if placed correctly. The sound of a generator running in the outdoors or late at night in a camping area can be exceedingly irritating, and in many places it is outlawed. It has a tendency to irritate some people.
To determine if this is the best option for you, calculate how much it will cost to run the generator. An ordinary generator will cost about $1 per hour to run; if run for 6 hours every day for a year, the cost will be around $2000, excluding fuel expenditures. The cost of maintenance and repairs would be added on top of that. With the strategy illustrated above, you would just about break even after twelve months at that price. If you only operate it for an hour or two a day, the payback time (in terms of money) will be longer. The noise, bother, and pollutants that generators produce are often considerably more important to many people than the cash cost - despite the fact that current generators are much quieter than older ones. Many sites, especially in the evenings, have restrictions on the use of generators.

Tips to Minimize Cost of Utilities

1. Slow Your Travel Planning Down

Staying in one spot for longer periods of time lowers the cost of full-time RV life. The cost of gasoline or fuel can quickly deplete your RV budget.
Furthermore, if you are paying for a campsite at a campground, you will often find that if you stay for at least 1 week (typically 1 night free) or even 1 month, you will receive a discount (1 week free).

Even if you plan on boondocking or dry camping on BLM land, staying longer will save you money on petrol to get to your next location.
If you want to stay in the warmer states throughout the winter, plan ahead so you don't have to pay expensive fees for last-minute reservations.

2. Slow down on the HIGHWAY

Slowing down on the highway can not only make you safer in your RV, but it will also save you money on petrol or diesel. It's a straightforward approach to save money while traveling in your RV.

3. Buy Only the RV Accessories you need to get started.

If you're new to RVing, try not to buy everything you see on the internet right soon. Start with just the RV accessories you'll need to get started, and then explore what more camper accessories you might need or want after a few weeks of RVing.
We have a lot of posts where we recommend some of our favorite products, but this is our major RV must-haves page.

4. Plan to do Free or Inexpensive Activities

When you get at your destination, don't feel obligated to see and do everything. Find ways to enjoy your time without going overboard on spending money you don't have. Purchase a yearly National Park pass and use it to visit many National Parks while hiking the trails. If you have a 4th grader, be sure to take advantage of the FREE 4th grade National Park pass, which allows your entire family to visit National Parks for the entire year. Find fun bike paths to explore with your kids if you have them and bikes.

5. Eat IN (or out of) your RV – Not at Restaurants

On a lengthy journey, it may be tempting to stop at a restaurant for a quick bite to eat. However, this is something you can prepare ahead of time to save money. Prepare your meals ahead of time and prepare to eat in your RV kitchen at a rest stop. You could even enjoy a picnic if the weather is great.
Having your own kitchen on your journey is one of the advantages of having your RV with you. Plan to use it on a regular basis so you don't have to spend additional money on eating out.

6. Use a Camping Membership

Consider purchasing a camping membership to gain savings if you live in your RV full-time and are seeking for methods to save money.

7. Find Cheap Gas Or Diesel

You can use the Gas Buddy app to assist us in locating real-time prices at gas stations as you travel. Before pulling off to an unknown gas station, make careful to check Google Maps' satellite view, as some are small and not designed for RVs.

8. Boondock – Camp for Free

If you have a good camping generator or solar panels and are prepared to dry camp, boondocking is a terrific method to save money while RVing.
There are numerous areas in the United States where you can camp for free for short or lengthy periods of time. You have the option of one-night camping in a Walmart parking lot or boondocking in a magnificent National Forest. If this is something you're thinking about doing, find out what RV dry camping basics you should acquire.

9. Visit Destinations in The Off-Season

You may always save money on camping fees and activities by traveling during the off-season. What about the shoulder season if you can't make it during the off season?
Fall, for example, is a fantastic season to visit Yellowstone National Park, and campgrounds just outside the park are significantly less expensive than in the summer.

To Tow or Not to Tow?

A tow vehicle—often referred to as a toad because RVers have strange names for things—is a major investment for RVers. Most travelers prefer or require a tow vehicle, whether it's a truck towing a trailer or an RV towing a car.

Towables

You'll need a vehicle or a heavy-duty SUV if you choose for a trailer or camper. The truck's size and model should be determined by the size and weight of your trailer. All of this information can be found in your owner's manual. If you don't already have a tow vehicle, I recommend purchasing the RV first. Instead of attempting to find a rig that will precisely work with your vehicle, you'll have more freedom to choose the appropriate house for you.

Make sure the GVWR (gross vehicle weight rating) of your trailer does not exceed the towing capacity of your car. I wish I didn't have to say this since it should be obvious. But it's worth repeating. Make sure the GVWR of your trailer does not exceed the towing capacity of your truck. The weight of your RV will increase as you add your stuff and fill up any of your tanks. If you simply consider your trailer's dry weight (or empty weight), you may tow a trailer that is 1,000 pounds heavier than you anticipated.

Another word of caution: it can be tempting to acquire a little trailer that can be towed by an SUV instead of a huge vehicle. Towing a trailer with an SUV incorrectly could cause your trailer to flip while you're driving. This recently happened to a friend of mine, and seeing photographs of his house strewn across the interstate was depressing. Pay special attention to your vehicle's towing capacity and trailer weight, and make sure the weight is distributed evenly in your trailer.

You'll need to find the correct hitch after you've chosen your rig and truck. Trailer hitches are available from your RV dealer or any auto parts store. If you go for a fifth wheel, you'll need a heavy-duty fifth wheel hitch installed in your truck bed. These are widely available and may be found at any RV store or dealer. You can find the correct sort of fifth wheel hitch for your truck on websites like etrailers.com. Towing tents and trailers is actually quite straightforward. Check your weight and invest in a good hitch. It's towing motorhomes that becomes difficult.

Motorhomes

You have greater towing possibilities with motorhomes. You won't need to tow anything with a Class B because they are normally tiny enough to fit anyplace (and their engines can't handle towing anyhow). It gets a little murkier with Class Cs and As. Should we acquire a tow dolly or tow four wheels down if we tow? What kind of tow package should we acquire if we're towing four wheels down? What is the cheapest option? What is the safest option? Is it necessary for me to pull a car behind my RV? For all RV towing scenarios, the last few years have provided an extensive trial ground. We've tried everything. We recently discovered the greatest setup for our ideal mode of travel: towing our 2002 Honda CR-V (automatic gearbox) behind our Winnebago "flat" or "four-on-the-floor."

Driving Without a Tow Vehicle or "Toad"

We drove our 1994 Class C motorhome across 48 states without using a tow truck during our first year of RVing. Heath was responsible for driving our rig through cities such as Austin, Los Angeles, New York City, San Francisco, and others.

The Benefits of Not Having a Tow Car:

- We saved a couple thousand dollars by not buying a tow package or tow dolly.
- Driving without a tow car was one less stress factor as a new RVer.
- We saved a few minutes of time when leaving campgrounds and arriving by not having to hook up a tow car.
- Better gas mileage.
- We saved a few minutes by not having to link to a tow car when departing and arriving at campgrounds.

The Downside of Not Towing a Car:

- If we wanted to visit major cities, we had to drive our RV into downtown areas.
- Trying to find a 29-foot parking spot was always stressful.
- Our RV was our only vehicle for errands. If we wanted to make a quick run to the grocery store, we had to pack up everything and move.

Conclusion: It's not fun driving a 29-foot RV in a city.

Overall, driving our RV without a tow vehicle was quite inconvenient. While it reduced the amount of work we had to do when packing up our RV to leave a park, it also added to our stress and limited our ability to do basic things like run to the store when we ran out of milk.

Plus, if there were any road restrictions, we had to avoid those areas entirely. For example, because the iconic Going to the Sun Road has a 24-foot limit, we missed it on our first trip to

Glacier National Park. We couldn't see the entire park in Big Bend because of another 24-foot restriction.

Driving RV With a Tow Dolly

A tow dolly is a trailer that allows you to tow a trailer with either your front two wheels or all four wheels on top of it. We only used a tow dolly for one day in west Texas in 2014 before abandoning it (long story), but we tried again a year later with slightly better luck.

We liked the Tow Dolly because:

- We finally had a vehicle to explore local areas, without having to bring the RV along.
- The tow dolly was free since we were borrowing it from a family member. Tow dollies are quite expensive if you buy one new (and can be more expensive than a tow kit).

What We Didn't Like About the Tow Dolly:

- The tow dolly's straps were a constant source of tension. They had to be adjusted on a regular basis and would fall loose during travel.
- It took a lot of time to hook up the car to the dolly.
- It was a little unsettling to drive the automobile onto the tow dolly trailer. I've never driven it off the front, but that's something we've seen people do when using a tow dolly, and it's always scared me.
- I was constantly worried about the car falling off the tow dolly.
- If we remained at a campground for more than a week, it was difficult to locate a spot to store the dolly.

Conclusion: It was convenient to have a second vehicle, but the dolly was more trouble than it was worth.

The most significant advantage of having the tow dolly was having access to our vehicle. The tension produced by the difficulty of connecting and disconnecting the car from the dolly, on the other hand, was not worth it. I wouldn't have recommended one if it wasn't fully free to use. However, for many vehicles, this may be the only towing option (see your owner's manual for details). We'll keep driving our 2002 Honda CR-V until it dies because it can tow without a dolly.

Towing Flat Behind Our Brave

Heath fitted a Blue Ox Base Plate and Blue Ox Pull Bar so we could tow our 2002 Honda CR-V behind our Winnebago (I'll go over the rest of the towing hardware in a minute). We can tow our CR-V with four wheels down instead of dealing with the stress of driving an RV through huge towns or the worry of fiddling around with a tow dolly. We've driven thousands of miles with this towing system, and I wish we had done it from the start. I was concerned about the cost and complexity of connecting and disconnecting the car from the RV, but it only takes a few minutes to connect our Honda CR-V to the RV.

The Benefits of Flat Towing:

- It just takes a minute to hook up the car for towing (plus a couple minutes of running the engine).
- We have a much better turn radius while flat towing versus the dolly.
- I'm not worried about our car falling off the tow dolly and smashing into someone.
- It's a lot less worrisome now that we have a Brake Buddy auxiliary braking system that will pump the brakes when we're driving downhill and stop the car if it detaches from the tow bar for any reason.

Conclusion: Because we can't think of any disadvantages, towing flat behind the RV is our clear winner.

The ideal setup has proven out to be towing our Honda CR-V with four wheels down. The automobile follows the motorhome closely enough that it's easy to forget it's there (i.e., it doesn't bring any additional stress despite the fact that we're longer). Our CR-manual V's owner's has a straightforward set of towing instructions and restrictions that make the procedure go smoothly. The rules are straightforward. We can't go faster than 65 mph, and we have to run the gears through a certain sequence to grease the transmission before towing. We must repeat the cycle if we drive for more than eight hours in a single day, which we never do.

How We Picked a Tow Package

Blue Ox and Roadmaster are two of the most well-known tow bar manufacturers. After reading several internet forums that compared the two companies, they appeared to be very equal items. Blue Ox was liked by some, while Roadmaster was preferred by others. As far as we could tell, there aren't many differences between the two tow bars. We chose Blue OX since we were on a tight deadline and couldn't find a local dealer who could deliver all of the parts on time.

Note that neither company sells directly to the public. You'll have to search their website or Amazon for a local dealer. We went with Amazon because it was the cheapest option and we love Prime two-day shipping.

What We Had to Buy for Flat Towing

Before we could set up our Honda CR-V for flat towing, we needed to purchase several different components. The following is a list of major purchases we had to make:

- Blue Ox Alpha Tow Bar

This tow bar attaches to our RV's trailer hitch and can tow up to 6,500 pounds. This is the most expensive component of your towing arrangement (prices range from $500 to 750 dollars depending on where you get it).

- Blue Ox Base Plate

When towing, the base plate will be put in your car and connected to the tow bar.

Note: Your vehicle's model and year must be specified when ordering base plates. If you shop on Amazon, you can use their filters to make sure you don't order the wrong part. We needed to find a base plate that matched the specifications of my 2002 Honda CR-V. We couldn't find a vendor on Amazon, so we spent roughly $320 for this part from a local dealer. Most dealerships charge several hundred dollars for base plate installation, but we were fortunate to have a knowledgeable friend who was ready to assist Heath. They spent three days drilling holes on our CRV's frame, removing our front bumper, studying YouTube videos for instructions, and putting the base plate back on. Blue Ox also included step-by-step instructions for mounting the base plate to the front of our CR-V, which were quite useful. You can save a few hundred dollars by doing the installation yourself if you have a few days and don't mind a little manual labor.

- Blue Ox light kit

To ensure that your tow car lights are attached to your motorhome, any light kit from an auto parts store will suffice. We acquired the Blue Ox light kit to make things simple and ensure that everything worked properly. It was about $45.

- Brake Buddy Towed Car Braking System

Auxiliary braking systems are meant to stop your car while it is being towed. As a result, when you hit the brakes in your RV, it also hits the brakes in your car. This will allow you to slow down more quickly and effortlessly. If, by some miracle, your tow bar fails or is utilized incorrectly, allowing your automobile to become detached from your RV, the Brake Buddy will engage your brakes and stop your car.

Towing does not always necessitate this. Many states have towing laws that dictate whether or not an auxiliary braking device is required. You can find a complete list of those restrictions, broken down by state and province. We got one for the added peace of mind it provided when towing and so we'd have one on hand if we ever needed one. (I'm picturing us speeding down a mountain pass when a deer darts out into the road—you'll need that extra stopping strength!) When it is an extra step to set up while towing, the sense of security overcomes the inconvenience.

The supplemental braking technology we utilize, Brake Buddy, will set you back $1,000 or more. We were able to save a few hundred dollars by purchasing ours used on eBay. It's somewhat expensive, but knowing that if something goes wrong, the Brake Buddy will take control of the vehicle makes us feel much better.

Before you buy anything.

This is an excellent opportunity to read the owner's manual for your vehicle. That doesn't sound like a bad way to spend an afternoon, does it? Every car can be towed in some form, and the owner's manual will show you how. The majority of people, including us, prefer to tow "four-on-the-floor." Before attempting this option, double-check your manual. Not all automobiles can be pulled four on the floor in a safe manner. If your automobile can't be hauled flat, you can tow it using a dolly (with two tires up) or a flatbed trailer (with all four tires up), depending on your vehicle's manual. A tow package (base plate + tow bar + lights) costs at least $1,000 without the optional Brake Buddy system, and a tow dolly costs similarly or more. Choose the option that is most appropriate for your car.

How to Find Free Camping

It's possible that RV parks aren't for you. After a summer of touring RV parks, I know I'm ready for some open space and boondocking. Let's go over some RV camping terminology you'll hear a lot before we get into locating free camping:

- Dry camping: You can camp here with no hookups, which means you won't have access to shore power, water, or sewer. When camping in state or national parks, the term "dry camping" is commonly used. You'll almost certainly have to pay fees if you're dry camping.
- Boondocking: Depending on who you ask, the definition of boondocking varies. There are a few things to consider:

1. You must be camping in a dry location.
2. It is completely free. You can camp at Walmart parking lots, rest spots, or in the driveways of friends.
3. (Debatable) You're in the wilderness or on free public lands, away from other people or RVers.

- Moochdocking: This is where you can camp for free on driveways or private land owned by a friend, relative, or, who knows, maybe you just like staying with strangers. You might or might not have access to electricity or running water. Many individuals enjoy boondocking and dry camping because it allows them to save money while also getting closer to nature. Because RV parks can be congested and noisy at times, we prefer to go dry camping or boondocking when we need a break from the crowds. If you recall from chapter two, this is when you'll want to make sure your rig is powered by a generator or solar power.

RV Sewage System

When you go from wood and bricks to an RV, you become acutely aware of your water, energy, and sewer usage. We've put up a simple beginner's introduction to the RV septic system in the hopes of removing some of the mystery for first-time campers.

Sewer repair is a hands-on task that isn't as frightening as it may appear at first.

To begin, there are three sorts of water:**fresh, gray, and black**. Water that is pure and safe to drink is referred to as fresh water. Gray water drains from your kitchen and bathroom sinks, as well as your shower drains. The sewage from the toilet is contained in black water.

Having the correct equipment and understanding how to properly repair your tanks can aid in the smooth operation of your journey.

Fresh Water

A normal garden hose can be used to connect a campground spigot to your city water hookup or fresh water tank on the side of your RV. Choose a 50-foot hose if you'll be camping somewhere with a long distance between water hookups. When we arrived at a few of state campgrounds where the water and power connections were at opposite ends of the campsite, we regretted buying the 25-footer. Because we had to park the RV near the water hookup, we were unable to fully utilize the camping space. A fantastic option is this 50-foot Zero G flex hose.

You'll want to get an insulated (heated) hose like this if you're going camping in a chilly region.

A spigot-mounted water pressure regulator protects your hoses and piping from high-pressure city water. We also bought an RV water filter, a connector splitter adaptor that allows us to use the outside spigot if necessary, and a 90-degree hose elbow that connects to the RV connection directly.

Gray Water

Food particles and bacteria from sink and tub/shower drains can be found in gray water. To maintain the sink drains as clean as possible, we aim to catch as much residue as possible from dirty dishes. We properly scrape dishes and use the drain trap to catch the majority of the remaining particles that could cause jams later. Some RVers are far less cautious.

Two different holding tanks can be found beneath the RV. - One is for gray water and the other is for black water. The two tanks have independent valves that open and close, and the water will flow through a single main exit valve.

You may be able to discreetly (and legally) eliminate small volumes of gray water straight on the ground depending on where you are camping or boondocking in rural places. If a campsite sewer hookup is available, that is the simplest option.

Note: We leave the gray tank open until a few days before our departure date from a campground. In the following part, we'll go over this in greater detail.

Black Water

Actually, unless you have a strong aversion to working with septic, the process isn't nearly as bad as it appears.

To connect from the hookup to your RV, you'll need a 20-foot hose. For those locations when the connection is a "mile" distant, we purchased a handy sewer hose kit that comprised two 10-foot hoses with swivel connections that join together. The transparent elbow that fits straight into the sewage connection in the ground is also included in the package.

The Sidewinder RV sewage support gives the sewer hose a beautiful downward slope and is a must-have for keeping all of the black water flowing smoothly into the sewer connection. In some areas, sewer supports are required because municipal rules restrict sewer hoses from touching the ground. We prefer the Sidewinder because it collapses effortlessly and has a storage grasp handle, so you don't have to fumble with an extra bag or storage container that you have to clean.

How Often to Empty RV Holding Tanks

The frequency with which you empty your black tank will vary depending on how often you use it. It usually amounts to 1-2 times each week for us. Many RVs include computerized sensors that can tell you how much water is in your fresh, gray, and black tanks. Unfortunately, you can't always rely on these since black water gets caught on the sides of the tanks and confuses the sensors. When in doubt, I simply press the toilet flush button and shine a flashlight down the dark hole!

We keep the black tank's valve locked until it's time to empty it. To do so, tighten all hose connections between the tank and the sewer tank, then turn off the valve. To do the task, you'll need a nice pair of disposable nitrile gloves.

How to Prevent RV Septic Clogs

- Make use of a Black Tank Rinser

This sewer tank rinser is one of the best investments we've made to keep our black tank and lines clean. It attaches to your RV's sewer outlet and has a hose connection that allows water to be sprayed directly into the tank. Pick up a spare tank-cleaning hose to keep in your sewer storage box for this purpose. Because the rinser is transparent, you can see when the water in the tank is clear!

- Use Enough Water

Allowing a proper amount of water to fill the toilet bowl before each flush is an excellent method to help prevent clogs. It's also a good idea to use toilet paper sparingly.

- Try Liquid Fabric Softener

On the day we leave the campground, we usually use the tank rinser to empty the black tank. Aside from that, we occasionally pour a little amount of liquid fabric softener into our tank through the toilet to produce slippery surfaces that can aid dislodge stuff caught on the black tank's walls. It also aids in odor neutralization.

- Use the Motion of Travel Days to Your Advantage

Before leaving, you can add some water to the black tank and let it to splash around inside the tank, breaking up any stuck-on solid waste. On travel days, we've heard of RVers emptying a bag of ice into their black tank through the toilet, but we haven't tried it yet.

Storing Your RV Septic Supplies

All of the sewage components (hoses, fittings, tank rinser and backfill hose, etc.) are kept in one of the compartments in a storage bin. We purchased our storage containers from Walmart and they are produced by Sterilite. We keep freshwater goods in one container and black tank materials in another. Don't put the two together in the same place! The size of storage boxes you choose will be mostly determined by the dimensions of your storage compartments, so take measurements before going shopping.

***A word of caution:** The exhaust fan does a fantastic job of ventilating the RV bathroom. However, do not flush the toilet while the fan is on. If you don't want the fumes from the black tank to get into your camper, don't do it. Yes, we had to learn that lesson the hard way right away.*

Many campgrounds offer complete hookups (water, sewer, and electricity) for each campsite. This is the most practical choice. Other campgrounds (such as state parks) may just provide electricity and water. To make sure what's available, check websites or phone ahead. Many campgrounds have on-site sewer dump stations.

How to Empty the RV Septic Tanks?

Steps-by-step:

1. The day before you wish to empty the black tank, close the grey tank valve.
2. Make sure the bathroom fan is turned off when you're ready to empty it.
3. On the outside of your RV, open the black tank valve. Wait until it's completely drained.
4. Using the Rhino Blaster tank rinser, refill the black tank (leave rinser valve closed).
5. Release Rhino Blaster valve.
6. Repeat until water runs out clear.
7. Close black tank.
8. Open the grey tank to drain the grey water and flush out your sewage hose. Keep the grey tank door open.
9. Optional: To avoid black tank odors and obstructions, flush the toilet with a sewer tank pod or liquid fabric softener and a few flushes of water.
10. When you need to empty the black tank again, repeat the process.

Note: Keep a close check on the water level when backfilling your black tank. Some RVers, I've heard, use a timer or have a spouse keep an eye on the level from the inside. I wouldn't base my decision on the RV sensors. Since we bought our camper, ours has been sporadic. I've heard horrible stories from visitors who left their campers unattended during this process and flooded them or destroyed their tanks.

Bonus tip: Close the gray tank valve a few days before you want to empty your black tank to give the gray tank enough time to fill up. Close the black tank valve after emptying the sewage and then release the gray water to essentially "flush" out your sewer hose before unhooking everything. It's not a replacement for cleaning your black tank on a regular basis, but it does help with the odor.

RV Electrical System

So let's assume you'll ALWAYS park where you can plug your equipment into an electrical outlet. Then we'll take it from there.

Is your RV a 30-Amp or 50-Amp model?

Every RV now comes with a power cord that can be used to connect to a campsite electrical pedestal like the one shown below.

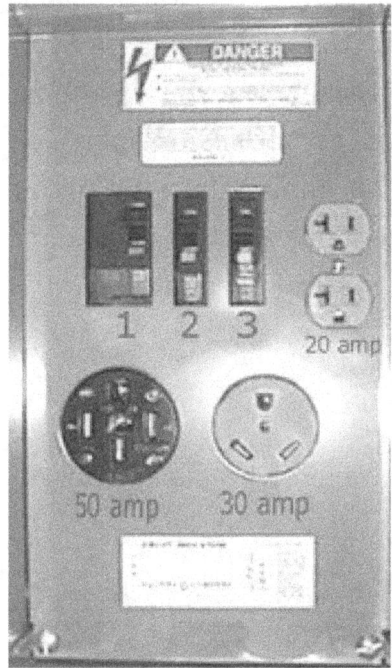

Your RV will either be a 30-Amp or a 50-Amp model. How did you figure that out? The most straightforward technique is to inspect the plug on your power cord. It is 30 amps if it is a big plug with three prongs. It is 50 amps if it is a big plug with four prongs.

Examine the power receptacles on the camping pedestal image above once again. The huge, circular three-prong receptacle will be 30 amps, while the four-prong receptacle will be 50 amps. The other two, the receptacles that appear like they belong in a house, will be 20 amps (or possibly 15 amps).

We don't need to go into amps in this section because it's so fundamental. Here's everything you need to know about it.

You can hook in and run practically every device in your rig at the same time if your primary RV power socket is four prongs (50 amps), including two air conditioners.

You can run one air conditioner and a few other appliances at the same time if your primary RV power plug is three-prong (30 amps). You might be able to run two high-efficiency air conditioners at the same time if you have two high-efficiency air conditioners, but not much else.

How do you figure out which appliances you'll be able to use? The appliances that generate heat or coolness (air conditioner, microwave, coffee maker, toaster, blow dryer, water heater, furnace, etc.) will require more electricity. You're more likely to trip a breaker if you run multiple of those items at the same time. Even I understand what breakers are, so I'll presume the bulk of our readers do as well. :) Many individuals utilize trial and error to figure out which objects can be used at the same time. They continue to turn on appliances until the circuit breaker trips. We'll go through how to use a little arithmetic to figure out exactly which items you can operate in the "Further Understanding Your RV Electrical System" section later.

Plugging In Your RV to The Campground Pedestal

You'll notice on the campground pedestal image below that there are four* breaker switches.

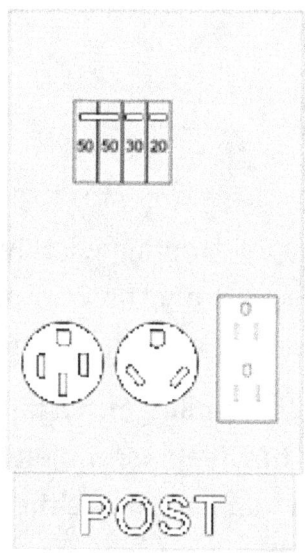

They should be labeled with 50, 30, and 20 (or potentially 15 instead of 20), as well as a description of which position is "off" and which is "on."

Two of the four breaker switches have the number "50" written on them. In "50 Amp Service vs. 30 Amp Service," we'll go into why this is.

The down position should always be "off," whereas the up position should always be "on," yet this isn't always the case. To add to the confusion, they are sometimes mounted side to side rather than up and down.

Before plugging in AND unplugging, ensure sure all breakers are in the "off" position for safety. When plugging in and unplugging, ensure sure all of your appliances, especially the ones that use the most electricity, are "off."

Of course, the camping pedestal may differ from the examples shown above. It could have any number of receptacles.

Simply plug in your power wire into the appropriate outlet. Turn on the breaker that corresponds to the receptacle. You can now use your appliances.

Electrical Adapters

So, let's say you have a 50 amp RV with a four-prong connection, but the park doesn't have a 50 amp outlet. Because this happens frequently, you should always have a 50 to 30 converter with you. The "dogbone" type adapter seen on the left is preferred by the majority of RVers. We like the "dogbone" look as well, but we prefer the more expensive Power Grip on the right, which has handles. The grips make disconnecting easier and, in my opinion, make this adaptor worth the extra money.

The four-prong receptacle on the adapter goes into your 50-amp chord, and the three-prong end of the adapter plugs into the 30 amp receptacle on the campground pedestal. You can then use your RV's appliances, but you'll be limited to the 30 amps provided by the power supply. As a result, you'll have to keep track of which appliances are running at the same time.

Some older campgrounds only offer 20- or 15-amp electrical supply. As a result, we stock both a 50 to 30 and a 30 to 15 adaptor, as seen below.

When we're at a campsite with only 20 or 15 amp service or when we're plugged in at someone's house, we use both converters simultaneously. Our power cord is plugged into a 50 to 30 adapter, then the three-prong end of that adapter is plugged into a 30 to 15 adapter, and finally into the pedestal. On 15 amps, we can't operate many things at once, but we can use our appliances.

What if you have a 30-amp RV and the campsite only offers 50-amp service (as we've seen before)? You can acquire a 30 to 50 amp adaptor, for example. This is something that a lot of people do and have never had a problem with. Basically, you'll have a 50-amp potential, but if you try to utilize more over 30 amps, your RV's 30-amp main breaker will trip.

This alternative does not appeal to me. It's done all the time, but there are enough dangers that OUR rule of thumb is to never connect to a power supply that is rated higher than our equipment.

Our fifth wheel is now a 50 amp unit. However, we are on 30 amps at least 50% of the time and frequently use our 50 to 30 amp adaptor. On 30 amps, we're perfectly good.

With that said, if you're looking for a setup to use full-time, we recommend obtaining a 50 amp rig. When you have 50 amps, you will have peace of mind and the power to run all of your appliances, and you can simply go down to 30 amps if necessary.

Checking Campground Wiring

This section might be placed before "Plugging In Your RV."

If you do a lot of internet research and read a lot of RV forums, you'll come across stories about people who have wrecked appliances because the campground's wiring was faulty or the voltage dipped below safe levels or surged above safe levels. Occasionally, you'll hear of folks being shocked (or worse) as a result of the campground pedestal's faulty wiring.

What are your options for dealing with this? One solution is to get a polarity tester and learn how to use it. This section might be placed before "Plugging In Your RV."

If you do a lot of internet research and read a lot of RV forums, you'll come across stories about people who have wrecked appliances because the campground's wiring was faulty or the voltage dipped below safe levels or surged above safe levels. Occasionally, you'll hear of folks being shocked (or worse) as a result of the campground pedestal's faulty wiring.

What are your options for dealing with this? One solution is to get a polarity tester and learn how to use it.

BEFORE plugging in your RV, you check the campground's circuit for adequate wiring. You contact the campsite management and MOVE to another site if your polarity tester indicates an issue.

The polarity tester no longer checks for incorrect voltage, which can damage your appliances. A polarity/voltage tester, such as the Good Governor illustrated below, is available.

You can use it to check the wiring as well as the voltage before plugging it in. The Good Governor, on the other hand, cannot continuously monitor voltage and cannot protect against electrical voltage decreases or surges. Drops or surges of this magnitude might harm your valuable appliances and devices.

As a result, we strongly advise that EVERY RV be fitted with a power management device, commonly known as a "surge protector with voltage protection."

These devices will keep your RV and appliances/electronics safe from the following threats:
- Surges
- Mis-wired Electrical Pedestals
- High & Low Voltage
- Other Miscellaneous Electrical Problems

They're available for 30-Amp and 50-Amp rigs (50-Amp models work on 30-Amp circuits as well). Models that can be plugged directly into the campsite pedestal and models that can be hard-wired into your motorhome are also available.

If you're using a portable model that plugs into a pedestal, all you have to do is plug it in and then plug your power chord into it.

You plug your power cord into the campground pedestal if you have the hard-wired model installed.

A two-minute delay is built into both models to preserve your air conditioner. It lights up and permits electricity into your equipment if everything is in working order with the circuits. No electricity is allowed in if there is a problem, and warning lights are displayed.

Notify the campsite administration and MOVE to another site if there is an issue. It's possible that you'll have to relocate to another campground!

The system protects the coach against surges once energy is admitted into the rig. It also turns off the RV's power if the campsite voltage falls below or rises above specific levels. This shields your appliances from harm.

The time delay prevents the air conditioner from cycling too quickly. When the compressor cycles on and off too quickly, it puts the compressor under a lot of strain and might cause damage. The time delay is just in case the air conditioner was "on" when you first plugged it in or if it was on during a power outage.

Every rig should include one of these devices, according to an RVIA Certified Master Technician, who suggested the SurgeGuard product (shown here). They're available for 30-Amp and 50-Amp rigs (50-Amp models work on 30-Amp circuits as well). Models that can be plugged directly into the campsite pedestal and models that can be hard-wired into your motorhome are also available.

If you're using a portable model that plugs into a pedestal, all you have to do is plug it in and then plug your power chord into it.

You plug your power cord into the campground pedestal if you have the hard-wired model installed.

A two-minute delay is built into both models to preserve your air conditioner. It lights up and permits electricity into your equipment if everything is in working order with the circuits. No electricity is allowed in if there is a problem, and warning lights are displayed.

Notify the campsite administration and MOVE to another site if there is an issue. It's possible that you'll have to relocate to another campground!

The system protects the coach against surges once energy is admitted into the rig. It also turns off the RV's power if the campsite voltage falls below or rises above specific levels. This shields your appliances from harm.

The time delay prevents the air conditioner from cycling too quickly. When the compressor cycles on and off too quickly, it puts the compressor under a lot of strain and might cause damage. The time delay is just in case the air conditioner was "on" when you first plugged it in or if it was on during a power outage.

Every rig should include one of these devices, according to an RVIA Certified Master Technician, who suggested the SurgeGuard product (shown here).

or a product from Progessive Industries (shown here).

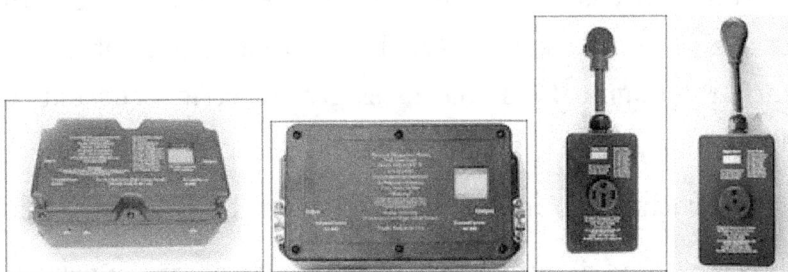

The "House" Or "Coach" Batteries

For the most part, all you need to know is what we've already covered. Your RV, on the other hand, relies on battery power to power certain lights and other appliances.

That happens all the time, but you should be aware of the battery system. One or two "house" or "coach" batteries are standard in most RVs. In contrast to the battery in a motorhome or tow vehicle that starts the engine, these batteries give electrical current to some appliances and motors in the RV.

House batteries must be recharged, and the most of them require minor maintenance.

You don't have to be concerned about battery charging if you are constantly plugged into an electrical outlet. A battery charger is included in your RV's equipment package, and it automatically charges the batteries using campground power.

Your house batteries are also charged in a different method, whether you have a motorhome or a towable (fifth wheel or travel trailer). The alternator in a motorhome charges your batteries while the engine is running.

If you're towing, the tow vehicle must be connected to the trailer in order for the trailer's brakes and lights to function. In addition, while you're going down the road, the tow vehicle's alternator is charging the trailer's house batteries.

When it comes to maintenance, ensure sure the battery terminals are clean and the water levels are maintained (only use distilled water in batteries). If you don't know how to do either, simply ask someone who has done it before or have an RV repair department do it for you. It's not tough, although getting to the batteries can be challenging at times. For the most part, all you need to know is what we've already covered. Your RV, on the other hand, relies on battery power to power certain lights and other appliances.

That happens all the time, but you should be aware of the battery system. One or two "house" or "coach" batteries are standard in most RVs. In contrast to the battery in a motorhome or tow vehicle that starts the engine, these batteries give electrical current to some appliances and motors in the RV.

House batteries must be recharged, and the most of them require minor maintenance.

You don't have to be concerned about battery charging if you are constantly plugged into an electrical outlet. A battery charger is included in your RV's equipment package, and it automatically charges the batteries using campground power.

Your house batteries are also charged in a different method, whether you have a motorhome or a towable (fifth wheel or travel trailer). The alternator in a motorhome charges your batteries while the engine is running.

If you're towing, the tow vehicle must be connected to the trailer in order for the trailer's brakes and lights to function. In addition, while you're going down the road, the tow vehicle's alternator is charging the trailer's house batteries.

When it comes to maintenance, ensure sure the battery terminals are clean and the water levels are maintained (only use distilled water in batteries). If you don't know how to do either, simply ask someone who has done it before or have an RV repair department do it for you. It's not tough, although getting to the batteries can be challenging at times.

What Happens When You Do Not Have Electric Hook-Ups

Our basic debate becomes more complicated due to the lack of power hook-ups. However, we'll keep it short and sweet.

You can use your appliances as if you were plugged in if you have a generator. A generator provides the same TYPE of power as a camping pedestal, but it's not quite that simple. The question is whether it generates as much power.

If you don't have a generator, you'll have to rely on your batteries to power the majority of your equipment. This necessitates the use of a "inverter." Inverters are found in some motorhomes and higher-end fifth wheels, although they are not found in most towable RVs.

Continue reading if you want to learn more about being without electrical hook-ups as well as the electrical systems. Otherwise, you have all of the necessary information.

Further Understanding Your RV Electrical System

As previously said, we began our RV lifestyle with a basic grasp of RV electrical systems. Actually, we didn't know much more than what was mentioned above. Despite this, we were able to hit the road and fully appreciate our RV's possibilities.

However, as time went on, we learnt a little more, and the new information has helped us to extend our horizons. So, below, we'll try to pass on some of that information. As previously said, we began our RV lifestyle with a basic grasp of RV electrical systems. Actually, we didn't know much more than what was mentioned above. Despite this, we were able to hit the road and fully appreciate our RV's possibilities.

However, as time went on, we learnt a little more, and the new information has helped us to extend our horizons. So, below, we'll try to pass on some of that information.

120-Volt Vs. 12-Volt

These days, every RV is built with both 120-volt and 12-volt power. What exactly does that imply?

The electrical pedestal at your campsite or, if you have one, powering your generator will give 120-volt power.

Batteries are used to generate 12-volt power.

The "force" driving electrical current through wires is measured in volts. Consider it in terms of water pressure. The more water that is pushed through, the higher the water pressure. The potential pressure is measured in "volts," and the actual pressure is measured in "volts." 120-volt power, obviously, pushes electricity through much more forcefully than 12-volt power.

Now, I was always perplexed when I heard the terms "110-volt" and "120-volt" systems used interchangeably. However, after doing some investigation, I discovered that they are virtually the same thing. Most of us don't need to distinguish between the two for practical purposes. I'll always refer to it as 120 volts because it simplifies the arithmetic we'll need to understand everything. You'll see what I'm talking about afterwards. These days, every RV is built with both 120-volt and 12-volt power. What exactly does that imply?

The electrical pedestal at your campsite or, if you have one, powering your generator will give 120-volt power.

Batteries are used to generate 12-volt power.

The "force" driving electrical current through wires is measured in volts. Consider it in terms of water pressure. The more water that is pushed through, the higher the water pressure. The potential pressure is measured in "volts," and the actual pressure is measured in "volts." 120-volt power, obviously, pushes electricity through much more forcefully than 12-volt power.

Now, I was always perplexed when I heard the terms "110-volt" and "120-volt" systems used interchangeably. However, after doing some investigation, I discovered that they are virtually the same thing. Most of us don't need to distinguish between the two for practical purposes. I'll always refer to it as 120 volts because it simplifies the arithmetic we'll need to understand everything. You'll see what I'm talking about afterwards.

AC Vs. DC

When it comes to RV electrical systems, there's a lot more lingo to learn. So let's see if we can make "AC" and "DC" more understandable. We all learnt this in elementary school, but most of us have forgotten it. Knowing the difference, on the other hand, becomes extremely useful and practical when RVing.

AC stands for "alternating current." That is to say, electricity can travel in both directions. To put it another way, imagine electricity flowing from right to left across a wire. Then it comes to a halt and reverses direction from left to right. It "alternates," stopping and beginning, changing direction, and moving in a wave pattern. Of fact, it happens so quickly that we are completely unaware of it.

"Direct current" is the abbreviation for "direct current." This indicates that electricity is only flowing in one direction. DC current is continuous because it constantly flows in one direction. The continuous current is beneficial for many appliances and motors.

Batteries generate DC (direct current). As a result, DC equipment such as lights and motors are powered by your RV batteries (your 12-volt system). The batteries, for example, provide power to motors that operate electric jacks and slides, hydraulic jacks and slides, and water pump motors. In addition, most built-in generators start or crank the generator using DC from the batteries.

The many currents are depicted graphically below. The AC current is at the top of the diagram, while the DC current is at the bottom.

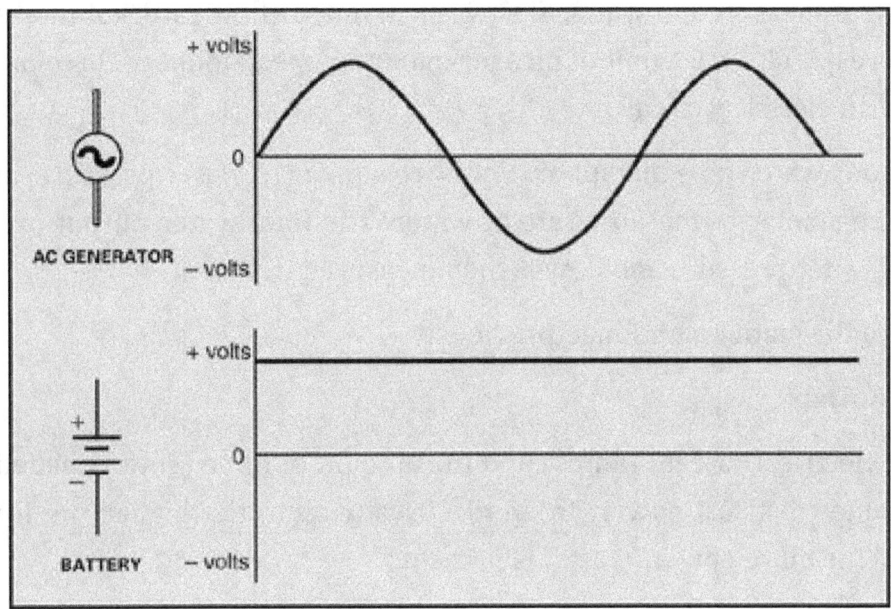

It's unnecessary to delve into the mechanics of how it all works. In the past, DC was the industry standard in the United States. AC, on the other hand, took over because it could be pushed over longer distances with more efficiency.

Those of us who have owned homes have never had to worry about the difference between "AC" and "DC." In stick houses, it's all air conditioning, and we never noticed the difference. We simply plugged things in and it worked. The only DC we used were torches and other small devices that relied on batteries.

In conclusion. Most of your RV appliances are powered by 120-volt AC power from the campground electrical pedestal and generators (TVs, microwaves, air conditioners, computers, blow dryers, satellite receivers, etc.) Your RV's batteries (sometimes known as "house batteries" or "coach batteries") provide 12-volt, DC power to non-AC appliances.

Volts, Amps, & Watts

Okay, I'm way out of my depth in this situation. As a result, I won't go into great detail to describe these concepts. However, knowing the link between volts, amps, and watts might help you figure out how much electricity you'll need to run your appliances.

Electrical power is measured in watts. Electrical current or flow rate/volume is measured in amps (or amperes). Volts are a unit of measurement for the amount of force or pressure that passes through an electrical circuit.

Let's return to our water pipe metaphor. Volts are similar to water pressure, as I previously stated. Amps are similar to the flow rate of water. The total water output produced by the combination of water pressure and flow is then measured in Watts.

Finally, I'll get to the math I mentioned previously.

Watts = Volts X Amps

The amount of electrical current (amps) and the amount of force (volts) needed to drive that current determine electrical power. In an electrical circuit, the higher the force (volts) or current (amps), the more power (watts) is present.

After a little math, we arrive to the following equation:

Amps = Watts / Volts

Why should we be concerned?

We're concerned because we need to figure out how much energy we'll need to keep our RV running. These math problems assist us in determining what our batteries can perform, what appliances we can operate at the same time in certain conditions, and what electrical system changes we might want to do in the future.

Because most of our RV electrical knowledge is based on amps, we typically need to know them. We connect to 20-amp, 30-amp, and 50-amp power outlets.

Volts are something we're always aware of. For RVs, it's either 120 or 12 volts, depending on whether we're talking about AC (120 volts) or DC (direct current) (12-volt).

Wattage is frequently available as well. It can be found on the nameplates of appliances or in the owners manuals. Alternatively, you can estimate wattage using one of the many online wattage tables for typical RV appliances. If you utilize internet tables, keep in mind that they are only estimates, as your actual appliances may differ.

50 Amp Service vs. 30 Amp Service

So, why can we run so many appliances at once with a 50 amp service when we couldn't with a 30 amp service?

Using our equation above, Watts = Volts X Amps, 50 amps creates 6,000 watts at 120 volts, whereas 30 amps produces 3,600 watts. That's a significant difference. But there's more to the story than that.

Remember how we said a 30-amp power line has three prongs at the start? Those three prongs are a hot 120-volt line, a ground wire, and a neutral wire, respectively.

The 50-amp power cord, on the other hand, has four prongs. A ground wire, a neutral wire, and two 120-volt hot wires are represented by those four prongs!

So, returning to our equation of Watts = Volts X Amps, we have two 50-amp lines, each at 120 volts. Not just one, but two lines, each capable of 6,000 watts. Our total potential power for 50-amp service is now 12,000 watts, compared to only 3,600 watts for 30-amp service. You can see why 50-amp service provides us with significantly more capability than 30-amp service.

A word about 50-amp service. Almost all RVs are connected with two 50-amp, 120-volt connections that are operated independently. In other words, some of the appliances are connected to one hot leg of the 50-amp service, while the others are connected to the other hot leg.

We also now understand why our pedestals have two 50-amp breaker switches, one for each hot line. Despite the fact that there are two switches labeled "50," they do not work separately. If one line is overloaded, the entire circuit will trip.

Finally, having a 50-amp surge protector with voltage protection on your 50-amp equipment is a smart idea. These devices test both 50-amp service lines and protect all of your appliances, regardless of which leg they are on. If you don't have one of these gadgets, it's possible that one faulty leg is the reason why some appliances operate while others don't. However, one injured leg will almost certainly lead to far more serious issues.

In a 50-amp circuit, the neutral is used to help balance the entire 240 volts between the two hot lines so that they each carry only 120 volts.

Figuring AC Electrical Requirements

Let's have a look at some instances of air conditioners.

According to the nameplate on our microwave, it consumes 1000 watts. The microwave would utilize 8.33 amps (1000 watts/120 volts) according to our Amps = Watts / Volts calculation.

Our toaster consumes 800 watts, which is 6.67 amps (800/120 volts).

Our living room television consumes 140 watts and draws 1.17 amps (140/120 volts).

1000 watts - 8.33 amps (1000/120 volts) are used in our coffee machine.

1875 watts - 15.63 amps (1875/120 volts) are used by Linda's blow dryer.

Our DVD/CD player consumes 80 watts and draws .67 amps at 80/120 volts.

3.5 amps for our refrigerator (they made that one easy and gave us amps instead of watts)

An RV water heater requires roughly 10 amps, a roof top air conditioner uses 13 - 15 amps, and an electric space heater uses 10 - 15 amps, according to our RV owner's manual. Any appliance with a heating or cooling element consumes a lot of electricity.

So we'll require 46.33 amps (15 + 10 + 3.5 + 8.33 + 8.33 + 1.17) if we run our air conditioner, have the water heater on electric (instead of gas), have the refrigerator on electric (instead of propane), and run the microwave, coffee maker, and TV. We'd best be on a 50-amp service or we won't be able to do it. :)

So, when you have AC power, that's how you figure out which appliances you can operate at the same time. Calculate the total amps by adding the wattages of each appliance. Then compare that value to the amps available from your power source (20, 30, 50). When using 30-amp service, you must obviously make more decisions than when using 50-amp service.

So, that's one way to figure out which appliances you can run at the same time. Trial and error is another option. Keep turning stuff on until the pedestal breaker trips, which is probably the most popular way among RVers.

When deciding what size generator to buy, it's also crucial to figure out how many amps each appliance requires. We were unaware of this when we purchased our rig, so we just answered, "Yes, give us the generator option."

We finally settled on an Onan 5500-watt gas generator. Our generator will produce 45.83 amps (5500 watts/120 volts = 45.83 amps), because generators create 120-volt AC power. So, with the generator running, we can basically run the same appliances that we could with a 50-amp connection. Until a neighbor tells us to turn it off or we run out of propane, that is.

Finally, a word on calculating amps and triggering breakers. When starting any appliance with a motor or compressor, an initial amp "surge" is common.

You can still trip breakers when you turn on a new appliance and add it to the circuit, even though your overall amp calculations, appliance by appliance, are inside the 30-amp or 50-amp threshholds. Allow for a small margin in your calculations to account for the start-up. Also, avoid plugging in multiple appliances at the same time. Let's have a look at some instances of air conditioners.

According to the nameplate on our microwave, it consumes 1000 watts. The microwave would utilize 8.33 amps (1000 watts/120 volts) according to our Amps = Watts / Volts calculation.

Our toaster consumes 800 watts, which is 6.67 amps (800/120 volts).

Our living room television consumes 140 watts and draws 1.17 amps (140/120 volts).

1000 watts - 8.33 amps (1000/120 volts) are used in our coffee machine.

1875 watts - 15.63 amps (1875/120 volts) are used by Linda's blow dryer.

Our DVD/CD player consumes 80 watts and draws .67 amps at 80/120 volts.

3.5 amps for our refrigerator (they made that one easy and gave us amps instead of watts)

An RV water heater requires roughly 10 amps, a roof top air conditioner uses 13 - 15 amps, and an electric space heater uses 10 - 15 amps, according to our RV owner's manual. Any appliance with a heating or cooling element consumes a lot of electricity.

So we'll require 46.33 amps (15 + 10 + 3.5 + 8.33 + 8.33 + 1.17) if we run our air conditioner, have the water heater on electric (instead of gas), have the refrigerator on electric (instead of propane), and run the microwave, coffee maker, and TV. We'd best be on a 50-amp service or we won't be able to do it. :)

So, when you have AC power, that's how you figure out which appliances you can operate at the same time. Calculate the total amps by adding the wattages of each appliance. Then compare that value to the amps available from your power source (20, 30, 50). When using 30-amp service, you must obviously make more decisions than when using 50-amp service.

So, that's one way to figure out which appliances you can run at the same time. Trial and error is another option. Keep turning stuff on until the pedestal breaker trips, which is probably the most popular way among RVers.

When deciding what size generator to buy, it's also crucial to figure out how many amps each appliance requires. We were unaware of this when we purchased our rig, so we just answered, "Yes, give us the generator option."

We finally settled on an Onan 5500-watt gas generator. Our generator will produce 45.83 amps (5500 watts/120 volts = 45.83 amps), because generators create 120-volt AC power. So, with the generator running, we can basically run the same appliances that we could with a 50-amp connection. Until a neighbor tells us to turn it off or we run out of propane, that is.

Finally, a word on calculating amps and triggering breakers. When starting any appliance with a motor or compressor, an initial amp "surge" is common.

You can still trip breakers when you turn on a new appliance and add it to the circuit, even though your overall amp calculations, appliance by appliance, are inside the 30-amp or 50-amp threshholds. Allow for a small margin in your calculations to account for the start-up. Also, avoid plugging in multiple appliances at the same time.

So Amps Are Amps, Right?

They are, in fact. BUT now we'll look at amps from a 12-volt DC perspective. Why would we want to do that when the majority of our major appliances run on 120 volts AC?

So, we could wish to park our RV somewhere where we won't be able to tap into an AC power supply. It's also possible that we won't have a generator. Alternatively, we may not want to operate our generator to generate AC electricity due to noise, fuel costs, or other factors. As a result, if we have a "inverter," we may use our 12-volt DC battery system to power AC appliances.

An inverter is a device that converts DC electricity to AC current by "inverting" it. Keep in mind, however, that in an AC environment, the electrical current is pushed through cables at 120 volts, which is ten times more than in a 12-volt DC system.

As a result, a 10-amp AC device necessitates 100 DC amps. This is supported by the formula we employed earlier.

We'll stick to simple math. Assume we have a 120-watt television. When connected to AC power, that equals 1 amp (120 Watts / 120 Volts = 1 Amp).

However, because of the lower voltage of the batteries, we would need 10 amps to watch TV using our batteries and an inverter (120 Watts / 12 Volts = 10 Amps).

To calculate the DC amps required to run the identical item using batteries and an inverter, multiply the AC amps required by ten.

You can see that when you're not connected to "shore power" or operating a generator, you'll need a lot of battery capacity to enjoy all of an RV's features.

Battery Capacities

Batteries for RVs are graded based on how many "amp-hours" they provide over the course of a 20-hour period. What's the big deal about 20 hours? I won't go into detail, but think of it as the number of amp hours a battery can supply in a day, from full charge to complete discharge (used up).

But what exactly does that imply?

Let's imagine we want to utilize our inverter and batteries for five hours throughout the day to power our two TVs, satellite receivers, a few lights, and two laptops (all hooked into AC plugs in the rig). Let's say we analyzed our total watts and determined that the appliances would require 5 AC amps in total. We know from our previous talk that using the batteries would require 50 DC amps (10 X 5 amps).

We could use 250 amp hours if we used all of those appliances for 5 hours (50 DC amps X 5 hours). As a result, a battery bank with a total capacity of at least 250 amp hours is required.

But it isn't quite that simple. We don't want to deplete our batteries more than 50% if we want them to survive as long as feasible (and less if possible). In our scenario, a battery bank with a capacity of at least 500 amp hours is required.

Most RVs don't come with such a massive battery bank as standard equipment. Furthermore, most RVs only contain one or two batteries with a total capacity of 100 to 200 amp hours.

Cost-cutting is always a priority for RV makers. Despite the fact that most mid-range and above RVs are supposed to be "self-contained," it appears that the industry assumes that all RVs will always be plugged into shore power.

So, if we want to update the rig's poor battery bank, let's have a look at our possibilities.

Battery Types

Starting (or Cranking) Batteries and Deep Cycle Batteries must be distinguished.

Most automobiles utilize a starting battery to start their engines. They're made to deliver rapid, intense bursts of energy, but they're not meant to be used repeatedly.

Deep cycle batteries are made to be discharged and recharged multiple times while providing energy for a long time. Deep cycle batteries may be discharged to around 20% of capacity and recharged multiple times (but they won't last as long if discharged that deeply over and over).

The many types of Deep Cycle Batteries will be discussed in the next section.

There are hybrids that are designed to start motors and offer long-term energy as well. They're primarily employed in marine applications. The hybrids, according to most experts, are NOT the batteries for your RV's electrical batteries.

Just make sure your house batteries are Deep Cycle and not Starting or Hybrid (commonly known as "dual purpose") Marine batteries. Starting (or Cranking) Batteries and Deep Cycle Batteries must be distinguished.

Most automobiles utilize a starting battery to start their engines. They're made to deliver rapid, intense bursts of energy, but they're not meant to be used repeatedly.

Deep cycle batteries are made to be discharged and recharged multiple times while providing energy for a long time. Deep cycle batteries may be discharged to around 20% of capacity and recharged multiple times (but they won't last as long if discharged that deeply over and over).

The many types of Deep Cycle Batteries will be discussed in the next section.

There are hybrids that are designed to start motors and offer long-term energy as well. They're primarily employed in marine applications. The hybrids, according to most experts, are NOT the batteries for your RV's electrical batteries.

Just make sure your house batteries are Deep Cycle and not Starting or Hybrid (commonly known as "dual purpose") Marine batteries.

Deep Cycle Battery Options

Wet Cell (or flooded cell), Gel Cell, and AGM are the three most common Deep Cycle Battery types (absorbed glass mat). I won't get into the technical differences between various types of batteries, but they're all lead acid batteries. Instead, I'll share links to several extremely useful websites.

The most frequent type of battery used in RVs is the wet cell battery. This is because they are less expensive than Gel Cells and AGMs. Furthermore, because RV manufacturers want to save money wherever they can, house batteries are usually Wet Cell, and the battery bank is usually insufficient unless the RV is always parked with electricity hook-ups.

Wet Cell batteries cost two to three times as much as Gel Cell and AGM batteries. For the same price, AGMs outperform Gel Cells, and AGMs are gradually replacing Gel Cells in RV applications.

The majority of the sources listed above appear to agree that AGMs are the best option. For many consumers, however, the cost difference between Wet Cells and Dry Cells is difficult to justify. If money isn't an issue when building a battery bank, I'll agree with the experts and recommend AGMs. Wet Cells will suffice in all other cases.

12-Volt Batteries Or 6-Volt Batteries?

One or two 12-volt batteries are standard in most RVs. Experts agree, however, that 6-volt batteries are preferable IF you have the space. They're bigger than 12-volt batteries of comparable capacity. "With similar capacity" is the important phrase in that sentence.

Experts also believe that connecting two 6-volt batteries in "series" (essentially generating a 12-volt battery) allows for longer discharge durations and better capacity than connecting two 12-volt batteries of same size. Two 6-volt batteries (connected in series to form a 12-volt battery) have more capacity than two 12-volt batteries of equal size.

To "produce" a 12-volt battery, two 12-volt batteries are placed in "parallel" (on the left) and two 6-volt batteries are wired in "series" (on the right).

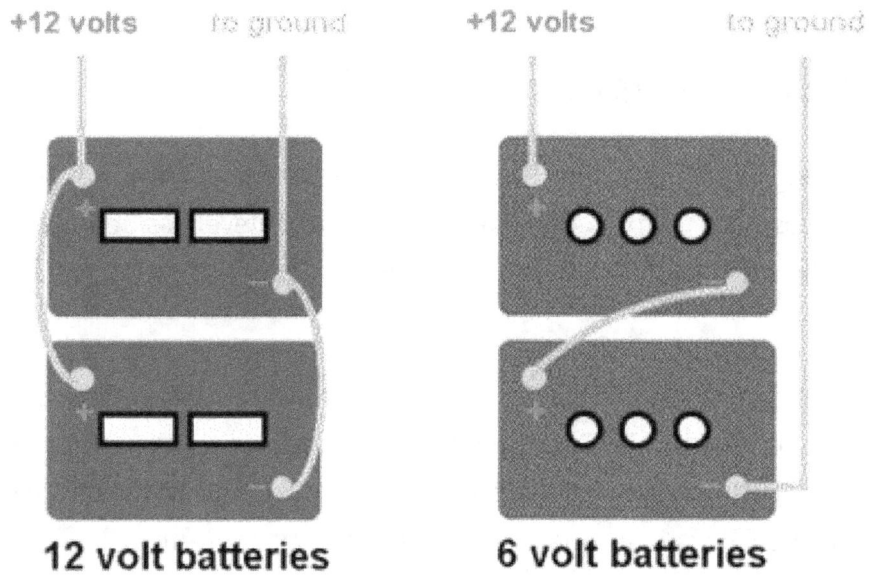

One more time, I'll trust the professionals. If space isn't an issue and you're changing or upgrading batteries, I'd choose two 6-volt cells wired together over a single 12-volt battery. NOTE: When people say you should place "golf cart" batteries in your RV, they're referring to 6-volt deep cycle batteries connected in "series." Okay, by this point, you've either decided that the whole electrical system/battery thing is too complicated and that you'll just park with electric hook-ups all the time **OR** you're starting to add up the amps of your appliances and calculating how many batteries you'll need and what kind/size you'll need to avoid using

Discharging & Recharging Batteries

If you've read thus far, I'm presuming you're interested in using batteries and an inverter, as well as parking without power hookups on occasion.

You have a few options at this stage.

- You can use the data above to determine what your present system is capable of and how to best utilise it.
- You can use the data above to figure out what you'll need to improve your current system.
- You can toss out your present setup and start fresh.

NOTE: When I say "upgrade," I'm referring to the batteries being completely replaced. It's better to have a battery bank with the same kind, size, and age of batteries.

As previously said, if you do not totally deplete your batteries, they will live longer. You shouldn't discharge them below 75 percent of their capacity, and certainly not below 50 percent.

If there's one thing I've learnt about deep cycle batteries, it's this: Each battery has a set number of discharge/recharge cycles, and draining the batteries too far too often reduces the number of cycles (and thus the battery life expectancy).

However, how do you know how far they've been released? Unless you have a battery meter, you won't know. We didn't have one of those in our rig.

The primary idea of this section is that you should at least twice the quantity of DC amp hour capacity you require. You'll be less likely to drain your battery bank below 50% this way. Naturally, if you quadruple the size of your system, you'll be less likely to overcharge the batteries.

However, there is a fine balance to be drawn between purchasing too much capacity and having enough to keep the batteries in good working order for as long as feasible. It's a difficult situation.

If you don't obtain enough capacity, you won't be able to live the way you want to without hook-ups. Alternatively, if you do operate all of your appliances, you may drain the batteries too quickly, shortening their lifespan.

Alternatively, you could acquire too much capacity and end up spending too much money. Another reason why many people prefer Wet Cell batteries is because of this. It's not as expensive to make sure you have adequate capacity, and if you do, you're not wasting as much as with AGMs.

Battery Charging

Well, if you're going to have hook-ups all the time, you won't have to worry about the house battery (ies). Your battery will be charged automatically whenever you have an electric connection. Almost every gear has some sort of built-in charger. The quality of that charge is determined by a few factors that we will cover later.

Most Popular Battery Charging Methods

A converter, an inverter/charger, or solar panels can all be used to charge RV batteries. While your RV or tow vehicle's alternator charges your batteries as you travel down the road, this is not the primary method of charging your batteries. Other charging options, like as wind power, are also available, but we'll focus on the three most common.

NOTE: The charging needs for different types of deep cycle batteries, such as wet cell, gel cell, and AGM, vary. As a result, it's critical to ensure that whichever charging technique you choose is appropriate for the sort of batteries you have and/or that your charger is properly set for those batteries.

Converters

Almost every towable RV comes equipped with a converter. It "converts" (transforms) AC electricity into DC power. The converter charges the batteries as well as providing power to the DC appliances.

If you're at a campground and plug into an electrical pedestal, the converter will automatically charge your batteries and run your DC equipment. If you are not connected to "shore power" but are using your generator, the converter will continue to charge your batteries and run DC equipment.

While the converter that comes standard in most RVs is functional, most electrical experts agree that it is not the greatest technique for charging your house batteries. In truth, that is most likely an exaggeration.

Standard converters are inept at managing the amount of charge that flows into the batteries, and thus can "cook" them. Batteries are finicky little things.

Furthermore, ordinary converters are just intended to keep the batteries charged. As a result, they're horrible at recharging deeply drained batteries.

Upgrade to a converter with multi-stage charging capabilities as an option. They are "smart" chargers that prevent batteries from being overcharged. External devices (such as the Charge Wizard brand) that plug into some existing converters to regulate battery charging are also available. While the converter that comes standard in most RVs is functional, most electrical experts agree that it is not the greatest technique for charging your house batteries. In truth, that is most likely an exaggeration.

Standard converters are inept at managing the amount of charge that flows into the batteries, and thus can "cook" them. Batteries are finicky little things.

Furthermore, ordinary converters are just intended to keep the batteries charged. As a result, they're horrible at recharging deeply drained batteries.

Upgrade to a converter with multi-stage charging capabilities as an option. They are "smart" chargers that prevent batteries from being overcharged. External devices (such as the Charge Wizard brand) that plug into some existing converters to regulate battery charging are also available.

Inverters
An inverter is a device that converts DC (battery) power to AC power, allowing you to use AC equipment in your rig without having to connect to shore power or operating a generator. An

inverter is common equipment on many motorhomes and some higher-end fifth wheels. Ours, however, did not.

Those RVs with an inverter will also have a converter, unless the inverter is a hybrid inverter/charger.

Again, the inverter that came with your rig might not have all of the features you want or need. This is another another reason why determining the wattage required to run the equipment you wish to run when not connected to AC power is critical. You can have all the battery capacity in the world, but you won't be happy if your inverter can't provide the watts you require.

The quantity of watts an inverter can give to your AC appliances determines its rating. To put it another way, a 3,000 watt inverter can give 3,000 watts of continuous electricity to a number of items.

Inverters also have a surge wattage rating that is higher than the continuous wattage. AC appliances, as you may recall, require a bit extra power when they first turn on, thus the inverter should be certified to withstand those surge wattages.

Both functions are performed by an inverter/charger. It converts AC to DC and DC to AC to charge batteries by inverting DC power.

It's better if the inverter/charger charger's section has a multi-stage charger that regulates the charge to the batteries. Multi-stage chargers give batteries a "bulk" (or boost) charge to get them to 75 percent to 90 percent capacity quickly. The charger then switches to a "absorption" (or regular) charge, which slows down the charge as the batteries near full charge. Finally, the multi-stage charger switches to "float" (or "trickle" or "storage") mode to top off and sustain the batteries without overcharging them.

I'm not going to get into the technical reasons why multi-stage charging is the best option for your batteries. That list could go on indefinitely. If at all possible, use a multi-stage or three-stage charger in your converter or inverter.

In addition, if you have a good inverter/charger and a good battery bank, you won't need a converter.

While we're talking about inverters, we should talk about the differences between pure (or true) sine wave and modified sine (or square) wave inverters. Huh? That's exactly what I stated.

Let's keep things basic for now. The utility company provides pure sine wave AC electricity to a house or campground pedestal (as indicated in the graphic in the AC / DC section above). It's a beautiful smooth up and down curve. The pure sine wave is preferred by all appliances.

Inverters with a higher price tag convert battery juice to AC power with a clean sine wave. Many inverters, on the other hand, convert battery electricity into a modified sine wave. The two wave shapes are depicted in the diagram below.

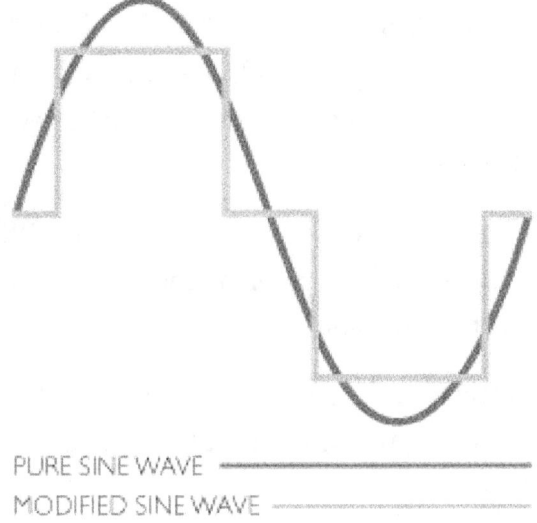

Modified sine wave inverters are less expensive than pure sine wave inverters and can power most AC equipment. That's why RV manufacturers prefer them over pure sine wave inverters, and why many consumers avoid them.

Modified sine wave inverters, on the other hand, can fry a wide range of electronic items, including laptop computers, medical equipment, laser printers, and other appliances. A pure sine wave inverter is the way to go if you want to be able to run all of your AC appliances safely.

Of course, if money is tight, a modified sine wave inverter will suffice. However, you must exercise extreme caution while determining which appliances are acceptable and which are not.

Full-timers should spend the extra money, if feasible, on a pure sine wave inverter, in my opinion.

SolarPanels

Solar panels are the quietest, cleanest, and cheapest (after initial purchase) way to charge batteries. Serious boondockers and those who want to park without hook-ups and without using generators prefer it.

Sunlight is free, unlike generator fuel (propane, gas, or diesel). Solar panels charge batteries without the use of noisy motors (as in generators).

Of course, you can't always count on bright, sunny skies, and solar panels aren't very efficient in the shadow. Solar panels, on the other hand, are highly expensive battery chargers. As previously said, they produce the cheapest energy once installed, but the upfront fees make recouping your investment difficult.

Many people believe that solar is difficult. I did as well. The difficult thing, though, is what we've previously covered on this page. The solar panel part is a piece of cake once you have a good battery bank and an inverter/charger.

Solar panels are essentially battery chargers. Sure, you'll need to work out what kind, size, and number of panels you'll need, but keep in mind that they're still just battery chargers.

Solar panels come in a variety of shapes and sizes. But that's not what we're going to talk about. They all function in essentially the same way. What matters is that you understand their output, how many you require, and how many you can fit on your roof.

Solar panels are measured in watts of output, and the larger they are, the more watts they create. They do, however, have volts and amps ratings. That's useful since we can use our Watts = Amps X Volts calculation to figure out what solar panels we could need or want.

Remember that we don't need to know output to power appliances; the batteries and inverter will take care of it. We only need to know output to ensure that we have enough panels to re-charge our batteries when we are not connected to the grid.

Calculating how much charging power you'll need in solar panels might be time-consuming. For every 100 amp hours of battery capacity, a reasonable rule of thumb is to get 100 watts of panels.

You'll also need a solar controller or regulator in addition to the panels. This is a gadget that connects your panels to your battery bank. The controller regulates the charge and ensures that the batteries receive the charge they require because solar panels can create more volts than the batteries can handle.

The beauty of solar is that you can gradually add panels. In fact, creating a full "boondocking" system can be done in stages. That is exactly what we did.

RV Electrical Wrap-up

That brings us to the end of our study of RV electrical systems. It was hoped that it was both basic and detailed enough to satisfy a wide spectrum of readers.

Our first goal was to demonstrate to newcomers like myself that they didn't need to know everything to get started.

Our second goal was to break down the language and processes so that even the most inexperienced individual could understand the basics and see how RV electrical systems are laid out.

Our third goal was to assist all RVers in either choosing their systems up front or modifying their existing systems.

Maintenance Routing Checks

- **Roof coatings should be inspected.**

For the most part, RV roofs are exposed to direct sunlight, and in some areas, snow covers them for part of the year. If preventative maintenance isn't done, a roof leak can cause serious damage to your RV.

Depending on the manufacturer, there are a few different roof coating options for RVs. Whatever type you have, it's critical to inspect it once a year for damage or degeneration caused by drying out.

Keep your RV away of direct sunlight as much as possible. Sealant will be placed around apertures and mounting hardware on roof-mounted equipment. If the sealant appears to be dry or missing, inspect it and replace it.

- **Check window and door seals**

Water leaks in an RV are one of the worst things that can happen. Leaks in walls and ceilings can go unnoticed until the damage has already been done. This can lead to structural damage to wooden materials used throughout your RV and of course, mold.

Before the season and before storage, do a thorough inspection of all window and door seals looking for dried out seals. Use a small screwdriver or something solid to check the area around these openings on the inside of the RV for soft spots.

Check for bubbles in the paint or discoloration. When in use, check for drafts around the doors and windows which would indicate poor sealing.

- **Perform RV water heater service**

We don't always need hot water, but we all desire it. The water heater in your RV is a simple technology that delivers a lot of convenience. Water heaters should be serviced at least once a year to keep them running well.

Drain and flush your toilet at least once a year. The best technique to completely clean the tank is to use a flush wand. While the tank is empty, inspect the condition of the anode rod if one is present. During the flushing, symptoms of rust or tank coating indicate a tank that may fail.

- **Service your wheel bearings**

We don't always need hot water, but we all desire it. The water heater in your RV is a simple technology that delivers a lot of convenience. Water heaters should be serviced at least once a year to keep them running well.

Drain and flush your toilet at least once a year. The best technique to completely clean the tank is to use a flush wand. While the tank is empty, inspect the condition of the anode rod if one is present. During the flushing, symptoms of rust or tank coating indicate a tank that may fail.

- **Continuously check your tires**

RV tires, more than any other item on our list, require the most preventative care. On days when you're traveling, you should check at least once a day. The cost of replacing a single tire may be minimal, but the expense of damage to your RV's undercarriage and sides as a result of a blowout can soon pile up.

Maintaining proper tire pressure is crucial, so bring a portable tire inflator with you. Tire pressure should be checked at least once a day on travel days, and ideally on a regular basis thereafter.

When feasible, keep tires covered and out of the sun, and consider using a UV tire treatment to help prevent the rubber composition from degrading. Always drive within your tire's recommended speed and load rating.

- **Be aware of humidity**

Humidity, another silent killer, is a concern with RVs that, if not addressed, can lead to significant issues. Some of the best camping spots are in hot, humid environments.

It's critical to have good airflow in your RV to avoid humidity build-up. When possible, open doors and windows to promote airflow.

Also, make use of your roof vents and fans. If you want improved two-way airflow, consider upgrading your roof vent. If you live in a humid location, an RV dehumidifier is a great method to avoid difficulties.

- **Provide sun protection**

We all adore the sun, but if you're not careful, it can be hazardous. The same can be said for your RV. Paint can fade, fiberglass can dry up, and decals can break when exposed to direct sunlight.

Many RVs feature elaborate graphics and paint jobs. Maintaining the appearance of your RV's outside surfaces can be time consuming, but the benefits are well worth it and will help maintain its resale value.

Waxing your RV once a year will assist to protect the paint and graphics. Waxing your RV also prevents bugs and road grime from sticking to it, making it easier to clean between excursions.

Consider using a cover for your RV while it's not in use and parked in shady places whenever possible.

- **Winterize your RV**

It's a pain to pack up your RV and store it for the winter, but it's also an excellent opportunity to undertake some preventative maintenance that can save you money when camping season arrives.

Make a to-do list. It's easy to park your RV and walk away, fantasizing about the next camping season. There are numerous small tasks to complete while winterizing your RV, so having a checklist can guarantee that nothing is overlooked.

- **Maintain your RV furnace**

We don't think about the furnace until it's time to use it. Furnaces are frequently left unlit for the majority of the season. In some circumstances, failing to use something might be damaging as well. Most RVers will have to deal with furnace repairs at some point, and they are typically hesitant to do so on their own.

Clean your furnace before the season begins. Electrical connections, sensors, and sensitive switches abound in your furnace. The operation can be harmed by dust, pet hair, and debris brought in by rodents. It's critical to get rid of anything that could jeopardize your furnace's safe operation.

- **Rodent proof your RV**

Who in their RV hasn't had an unwelcome roommate? Unwanted pests, whether mice or insects of some kind, can bring a slew of issues. Building nests within your furnace, removing insulation in walls and floors, and chewing wires can all lead to hours of hunting for an electrical issue.

Before storing your RV, check sure any wiring, gas lines, and other connections to the inside are securely secured. Sealing these places with spray foam is a smart option. Because spray foam dries out, make sure it's in good shape.

Many rodent and insect repellents are available on the market to assist keep unwelcome visitors away during storage and use. Another tried-and-true method for sealing holes where pests could enter is steel wool.

RV Maintenance and Repair

Good old Pappy Van has to be checked on from time to time! Well, not every time, so you do not need to be afraid. I will go straight to the point with this one. Things will surely break if you are RVing full-time. Be ready to incur the charges each month, as it may save you the many knockouts and headaches that may turn your RVing into another mayhem. You will need to be changing your tire and propane regularly. Just be prepared to spend about $50 to $100 a month. You may need to adjust this number, depending on the condition of your road van. Of course, worst case scenarios such as the fuel pump giving up or transmission throwing in the towel may come up and will have to take an emergency fund. For such cases, think about $500 to $200. But for normal monthly menace, budget about $100 tops.

Other Expenses:
We've gone through a few of the big ones, particularly those that having to do with RVs. Let's take a brief look at the others before moving on.
1. Groceries: $400.
2. Eat-outs: $100.
3. Phone and Internet: Check the Verizon section.
4. Health insurance: $250.
5. Utilities/Dump Fees: $30.
6. Laundry: $40.
7. Propane: $5.
8. Fun: Totally up to you.
9. Regular Living Expenses: Varies.
10. Miscellaneous: Nobody's business.

So How Much Does It Cost?

I mean, why are you still asking? Okay, I'll try to assist. The average cost of living in an RV for two people in a year is $10,000, according to studies from seasoned RVers.

While this may seem excessive, keep in mind that it covers EVERYTHING. Before you get too excited about the statistic, keep in mind that, according to careertrends.com, the average cost of living in the Midwest for a couple without children is $39,649! So you see that by racking up miles on the road and putting petrol in your RV, you are going forward while saving more than half of your money. EVer, you just saved a lot of money!

Chapter 4: The RV Life

RV Driving Safety Tips

Driving can be intimidating for new owners, whether they have a motorhome or are hauling a trailer. With a 44' fifth-wheel, I can assure you that I know what I'm talking about. With a little practice and patience, you'll be navigating parking lots, gas stations, and right turns in no time. Here are six pointers to get you started on your RV adventure.

Size Awareness

It's no surprise that towing a trailer or driving a motorhome has an impact on route planning. To begin, you must determine the height and weight of your car. Use an RV GPS device or Trucker Atlas to plan your trips, which can notify you of low bridges or other restrictions.

Consider maneuverability when considering potential routes. Is your path going to take you through a crowded city? Patience is required when merging and yielding. When driving in congested areas, you must be mindful of vehicles all around you, particularly in blind zones.

Finally, obtaining gas can be a challenge. Make careful you pick a gas station with enough of room to navigate around the pumps and parking lots.

Wide Turns Required

When it comes to maneuverability, you'll have to make wide turns. Because you'll be up against the curb on right turns, this is especially true. If you make a quick turn, your back tires may end up on the curb or tracking over someone's grass.

To avoid a collision, you must also stay in your own lane, therefore pull out further into the intersection before commencing the turn. Keep an eye on your rearview mirrors, stay as near to the center lane as possible, and be wary of impatient vehicles who may try to pass you by.

Take It Slow

There should be no need for speed when driving an RV or towing a camper. Take pleasure in the journey. This is due to a number of factors. First, braking will take a little longer with that much weight behind you. That grows tremendously with speed.

You'll also need to keep a bigger gap between you and the vehicles in front of you, stay alert, and give yourself enough time to react. Slowing down will also save you money at the petrol station. By lowering your highway cruising speed from 75 mph to 55 mph, you can save up to 20% on gas.

Maintain Your Vehicle

A safe vehicle is an RV or tow vehicle that has been well-maintained. Keep up with preventive maintenance and frequent inspections of your RV systems, particularly those that could cause an accident while you're on the road. Make a pre-trip checklist and go over it with your passengers every time you get behind the wheel:

- Belts and hoses (check for cracking)
- Headlights, turn signal, tail lights
- Hitch or towing equipment
- Tires for the correct air pressure and sufficient tread depth

One of the most common causes of RV accidents is tire blowouts. Overloading, under-inflation, or aging tires can all contribute to them. Avoid blowouts by double-checking your tires, driving at the proper speed, and making sure they're not overburdened.

Pay Attention to the Weather

Driving in bad weather is another significant cause of RV accidents. RV driving is dangerous in the rain, fog, ice, and especially severe winds. Plan your trip to avoid inclement weather, and allow extra time in case of delays due to unforeseen storms. If you're driving and the weather turns dangerous, pull over at a rest stop or the next exit. Please keep in mind that in the event of strong gusts, there is no better choice than to pull over to the side of the road and wait it out. Keep an eye out for debris and downed power lines when you go back on the road after a storm. It is never a good idea to drive across standing water. You have no idea how far down it could go.

Practice Makes Perfect

Before you go on a road vacation, spend some time practicing turning with your RV. Locate a large open parking lot or dirt field. Set up some cones and practice parking and maneuvering. Most importantly, don't be hesitant to seek assistance or enroll in a driver's education course. Spending some time getting to know your RV and its limitations will ensure a safe trip while also making it more enjoyable.

RV Insurance and Extended Warranty Plans

Rv Insurance

After you've purchased your RV, the first thing you'll need to do is purchase RV insurance and register your vehicle. This is a hard situation! Your vehicle must be registered and insured in the state where you live.

Insurance may be a big pain in the neck if you've been living for any length of time, and this is especially true when it comes to RVs. The most crucial thing to remember is this: Full-time RVers are not covered by all insurance companies. The operative word is "full-time."

If you intend to live in your RV full-time, you must inform your insurance agent. Full-timing is defined by insurance as spending more than six months of the year in your RV (but this could change at any given time). To make matters even more confusing, it's not uncommon for an insurance company to claim that they don't offer full-timer insurance when you know they do. You have the option of finding your insurance through Good Sam. They make the procedure considerably easier for newcomers by comparing several insurance companies and providing you with options.

They can be used for years, and many people are concerned about what will happen if their RV is in the shop and they are suddenly without a place to sleep. While most technicians would let you to stay in your RV overnight, many full-timer insurance plans include coverage for hotel nights. When we broke down just south of the Grand Canyon, we used this.

Roadside help is something you'll undoubtedly need on the road, and it's included in your insurance package. It is essential that you travel with it. One of the best is Good Sam's Roadside Assistance. It costs less than $100 a year and can come in handy if your tow dolly's tire blows out. Good Sam's Roadside Assistance will go above and beyond to help you choose the proper tire.

Getting Mail and Establishing Your Domicile

When people find you live in an RV, the first question they usually ask is, "How do you get your mail?" If you'll be full-timing, mail might be very difficult, and you have a few possibilities. First and foremost, you'll require a permanent address, which will necessitate establishing your residence.

- **Why you need to establish your domicile**

When you live on wheels and don't have a "permanent residence" in the United States, you'll need a permanent address for everything—RV parks will even ask for it!—which is problematic when you don't have one. Vehicle registration, voting, insurance, taxes (and so on) all require a permanent location, which is why you'll need to establish a domicile before you hit the road.

Your domicile is simply your new residence, and there are three major states that make excellent domiciles: Texas, South Dakota, and Florida are three of the most populous states in the United States.

- **Picking your domicile state**

You're in luck if you're already from one of these three RV-friendly states. That is how we came to decide on Texas. But it's entirely up to you which state you live in! Because regulations varies from state to state, here are some of the most important aspects to consider when deciding where to live:

- Taxes (Income, sales, vehicle, etc.)
- Vehicle inspection and registration laws
- Homeschooling laws (if you have kids on the road!)
- Driver's license renewals Jury duty

- **Where you plan to travel**

If the state you chose demands annual visits, where you plan to travel is crucial. Every year, we must travel to Texas to renew our vehicle inspection. This isn't a big deal because we see our families at least once a year, but it can be inconvenient depending on where you want to go.

- **So, how do you actually establish your domicile?**

There are firms that will set up your residence for you, and I strongly advise you to do so! You can borrow a parent's or a friend's address, but it will save you so much trouble in the long run if you establish your own legal domicile once and for all. (What if your pals decide to relocate? What if your mail is misplaced by your parents? What if they find it inconvenient to have to forward your correspondence to you on a regular basis?) This isn't a particularly costly procedure; it simply takes some time.

We advocate establishing your domicile with Escapees because they can set you up in any of those three states and provide much more than simply mail forwarding. If you want to visit Florida, St Brendan's Isle comes highly recommended.

Getting your mail on the road is simple if you've found a provider you like. Escapees, for example, will set up a domicile for you, provide you with a permanent postal address, and even forward your mail to you while you're on the road (while filtering out rubbish!). They've been in business for more than 40 years and know what they're doing. After you've set up your address, you'll be able to have a lot of fun altering your address on everything. You'll begin with government-related items such as your driver's license, vehicle registration, and so on, before moving on to bank accounts, bills, and insurance. I strongly advise using a service because they will provide you with a checklist to guide you through the procedure.

- **Getting your mail in your hands**

Set up mail forwarding with USPS to your new address once you've established your domicile and are moving out of your current residence. I had to pay a $1.05 identification verification fee for this. However, in an odd and unexpected twist, USPS offered me discounts for a list of firms I might need during my move as a thank you for forwarding my mail. This included a 10% discount on Amazon orders. This was an unexpected surprise as I set up my mail forwarding over the holidays.

As a result, I received $1.05 in Christmas shopping savings. You can arrange your start and finish dates for forwarding when you set up your mail forwarding (simply Google USPS mail forwarding and choose the "change your address" option). I set a start date a few days before I moved out (so I wouldn't lose any mail amid the chaos of moving into an RV) and labeled my move permanent, so my mail would continue to forward indefinitely. Your mail forwarding request will be handled and confirmed within 24 hours.

After that, your mail will begin to be forwarded to your home address. Once you've updated your address with all government agencies, your bank, any subscriptions you've received in the mail, and any companies that may send you tax forms, and you've set up mail forwarding from your previous address, you're ready to go.

Double-check that you've updated your address everywhere now that you've established a residence and forwarded your mail. Your bank, your insurance companies, any companies that may send you tax forms, any subscriptions you have, and perhaps even go old school and send an email to all of your friends and family announcing your new legal address.

Your mail will be forwarded, but it's important to keep your address up to date with banks, insurance providers, and employment.

You're free to travel the country after you have an address for all your mail! Now all you have to do is figure out how to get your mail while boondocking in Grand Teton National Park. If you want to use Escapees mail service, you have a couple options for roughly $100 per year (plus setup fees):

- You can have your mail opened and read to you by calling in.
- Mail scanning — Your envelope is scanned and emailed to you, and you can choose whether or not you want your mail forwarded to you.
- Mail forwarding — Give us your current mailing address and we'll send it to you. If you'll stay in one spot for an extended period of time, you can set this up to happen automatically.

"What if I'm not at my current address long enough to receive my mail?" you might wonder. I'll get to that in a minute. With having to figure out every single place where you need to update your address and filling out the appropriate papers, the actual process of changing your address and establishing your legal domicile is tedious and cumbersome.
(Though you'd still have to do all of that if you just moved down the street.) Getting your mail, on the other hand, is simple. It is possible to have someone read it to you. Alternatively, you can have it forwarded to you. Alternatively, you can scan it and send it. There are so many possibilities!

- **Receiving packages on the road**

The best invention of the decade and an RVer's best friend is Amazon Prime. We frequently send products to RV parks, and we've never had a problem with two-day shipping! If you need to receive a box while on the road, the most convenient option is to mail it to the RV park where you are staying. We normally notify the campground ahead of time that a package is on its way. They will accept your letter and notify you when it arrives. Our items were delivered to our doorway at our previous camper by the campground personnel. Simply ensure that your address label like the following:

Name of Campground

Attn: Alyssa Padgett Site #52

Address

City,ST Zip

And that's all there is to it! It's critical to provide your name so that both USPS and the campground receive your delivery. This is an important step to remember! If you're not staying in a campground or boondocking, you can have your box delivered to a post office or UPS store. While we were boondocking on national forest land in the Tetons, I had to spend $5 to pick up a box from the UPS store. The charge is inconvenient, but if you don't have a physical address to ship to, it's a viable choice. If you opt to ship to a post office, make sure your mail is marked "general delivery." Alternatively, consider this:

Alyssa Padgett

General Delivery

City, ST Zip

I prefer to have all mail and packages delivered straight to our campground so that they don't get lost in the shuffle. As I previously stated, we routinely use Amazon when on the road, and we've never had a box go missing or get misplaced (knock on wood).

The US Forest service

The United States Forest Service (USFS) campgrounds offer a variety of amenities to meet the needs of RV campers. Others have pit toilets and hand water pumps, while others have flush toilets, showers, and running water. Trash cans, fire pits, and picnic tables are almost always present. Camping fees range from zero to a few dollars. A camp host is available at many campgrounds. The majority of the 4300 USFS campgrounds allow stays of up to 14 days, but certain popular areas have a shorter limit.

Boondocking – Dispersed RV Camping

The US Forest Service refers to camping outside of a designated campsite as dispersed camping. The USFS encourages this form of camping, but there are some guidelines and advice to follow.

Finding Forest Service Campgrounds

The USFS manages nearly 4000 RV-friendly parks around the US. Finding many of these RV camping world's hidden treasures can be tough, as each forest has its own camping information. The Coleman USFS Campground Directory is the greatest tool we've discovered for finding USFS campgrounds. This comprehensive guide contains information on every USFS campground in every state. The number of camping sites available, the utilities provided (such as water, toilets, and trash), and any RV size restrictions are all included in this book. You'll be on your way to RV camping paradise if you combine this book with a good map.

USFS campgrounds can be found in a variety of locations, with some of the roads leading to them being small. Pop-up campers, tiny travel trailers and fifth wheels, and truck campers are best suited to more distant USFS campgrounds, which usually have well-maintained roads suitable for any size RV. That's not to say you won't be able to fit a large RV into any of these fantastic camping places, but you'll have to plan ahead. You don't want to drive up a logging road where you could have to turn around or back out.

US Forest Service Campground Reservations

If you're worried about not being able to find a spot to park your RV at a campsite, there are over 1700 Federal public land campgrounds with thousands of RV camping sites that can be reserved ahead of time. The majority of the reservation-required campgrounds are located in attractive regions, and the reservation system is available countrywide. You may plan your RV vacation and stay entirely at USFS campgrounds utilizing this unified reservation system, which requires only one web site for all reservations across the country. Popular campgrounds book up quickly, so make your reservation as soon as possible.

When you visit the Reserve America website, you'll see a map of the United States with campgrounds that accept reservations. By clicking on a region in the United States, you can "dig down" to specific campgrounds, which include a map of the camping area. You choose the dates you want to stay, and the system shows you what's available. You can book your RV camping spot with only a few clicks. There is no better way to locate public lands campgrounds that can be reserved.

RV Camping Maps and Navigation

The majority of RV camping information in our National Forests may be found on the internet. Our USA RV Camping Map or the US Forest Service Website have links to each National Forest. Official travel maps for each National Forest you wish to visit can be purchased on their websites.

Good detailed maps can assist you in locating USFS campgrounds that suit your RV camping preferences. If you're planning a trip to the western United States, we recommend the particular state Benchmark Recreation Atlases. There are two sections in each state atlas. A leisure section with roads and public land limits, as well as a shaded relief road segment. What we like about the Benchmark maps is that the roads displayed into public areas are usually appropriate for RV camping vehicle driving, and you can be relatively confident that you won't end up at a dead end if you head along a plotted road. Using the shaded relief portion, you may rapidly get a sense of the type of RV camping place to seek for. You'll soon come across regions that look interesting and lead you to some of the best RV camping spots.

The DeLorme Atlas & Gazetteer state series maps are another choice. Every state has one of these map books available. They provide more information than the Benchmark maps. These maps are used by the majority of experienced backcountry RVers. Backcountry navigation is made considerably easier thanks to the great level of information. Some back country mapping roads may not be suited for you or your RV, so be prepared to explore beforehand.

When choosing a campground, it's important to remember to consider elevation. High mountain places will have very cool nights and hot days, so dress appropriately. I can't tell you how many times we've assisted RVers with children who had forgotten to pack warm clothing for their camping excursion. If you're from a lower height, it's easy to forget that the mountains can be frigid and snowy in July.

RV Camping in The National Forest

USFS Campgrounds are great RV camping locations for several reasons:

- Scenic Beauty surrounding the campgrounds
- Roads reasonably well maintained for almost any size RV
- Primitive campsites are the perfect companion for RV camping
- Basic facilities at most campgrounds
- Most campgrounds are easy to find

The USFS and its contractors frequently maintain campgrounds in attractive locations. Great beauty, historical landmarks, and other outdoor leisure locations are all within a short drive of the campground. Although the roads leading to USFS campgrounds are well-maintained, they frequently necessitate driving on gravel roads. These roads are sometimes washed out. Some routes and parks are not suited for all types of RVs. Smaller RVs, such as truck campers and tow behind pop-up campers, are often best suited for remote USFS locations. It's wise to check with the local USFS Ranger District Office for road conditions or investigate the road before taking your RV.

USFS campgrounds are ideal for self-contained RVs since they offer a variety of amenities to make camping more comfortable. Picnic tables and fire rings are frequently provided. The most popular type of toilet is a pit toilet, however we stayed at a USFS campground in Colorado with solar-heated showers and flush toilets. Water is available at most USFS campgrounds, either through a hand water pump or a water spigot. Although there is generally a trash can, be prepared to take your garbage home with you. Some campgrounds are designed as loops, while others are "in and out" dead end spurs. The most frequent are loops. In the campsite, keep an eye out for low tree branches and tight corners where a tree or boulder could grasp the side of your RV.

If you have the Coleman USFS Campground Guide and a good map, you can find any USFS campground. Local USFS Ranger District Offices have maps and can provide you with the most up-to-date road and campground status reports for the area you're interested in visiting. They can also tell you about little-known facts about the area you want to visit, such as historic ranch and railroad buildings, mines, and other surrounding areas of interest.

USFS campsites provide a diverse range of excellent RV camping opportunities. You'll locate fantastic US National Forest RV camping sites if you choose and use your research tools correctly.

Heathcare options for Rvers

Does Health Insurance for RVers Exist?
Insurance for full-time RVers is one of the most prevalent subjects of discussion around the campfire. We all hope that we won't become sick when traveling, but we want to be prepared in case something unexpected occurs. And, to be honest, navigating the world of full-time RVers insurance can be a bit intimidating, especially if you've never had to do so before.

The majority of Americans are covered by their employer's health insurance. You probably won't need health insurance if you continue to work at your corporate job while on the road. In fact, our healthcare system was built on the concept of employers offering insurance as a benefit to their employees. It's still the easiest place for huge groups of people to get to (or, employees of a company).

Many of us who quit our jobs to pursue a nomadic lifestyle are freelancers or self-employed. We might run a modest firm on our own or with a partner, but we're certainly not a "big group" by any stretch of the imagination.

Don't worry if this describes you. You don't have to go without health insurance if you don't want to. Even better, obtaining affordable healthcare isn't quite as difficult as it may appear. In fact, folks looking for full-time health insurance have a variety of possibilities.

Health Insurance Options for RVers and Additional Resources

RVer Insurance Exchange

The RVer Insurance Exchange, in collaboration with the Escapees RV Club, is a great location to start looking into health insurance options for full-time RVers.
You can enroll with RVer Insurance Exchange and have an agent pick a plan for you if you find the whole process of looking on your own too stressful. They'll provide you a free quote and scan both marketplace (ACA) and non-marketplace plans to discover the one that best meets your needs.

Quick Guide to Shopping for RV Health Insurance – courtesy of RVer Insurance Exchange

In a word, these criteria are cost (how much do you want to spend?) and availability. & mobility (how far can you go without losing service?). In a word, these criteria are cost (how much do you want to spend?) and availability. & mobility (how far can you go without losing service?).

Affordability

- **Stay healthy:** The best advise for people of all ages is to exercise prevention: take care of your health to avoid significant problems later on. But we all know that even the healthiest of us can have problems that arise out of nowhere. Did I say something about "the Joe factor"? The best advise for people of all ages is to exercise prevention: take care of your health to avoid significant problems later on. But we all know that even the healthiest of us can have problems that arise out of nowhere. Did I say something about "the Joe factor"?

- **Share some cost:** The larger your deductible or out-of-pocket maximum, the lower your monthly premium will be. This could also allow you to "self-insure" by setting aside money for a rainy day.

- **Compare plans and carriers:** Details of healthcare plans are constantly changing, so it's a good idea to shop around. By shopping around for several providers, you might be able to obtain comparable coverage at a lesser cost.

Portability

- **Make sure the company you purchase an insurance plan from insures RVers:** Some insurance feature a rider that excludes RVers from coverage, which may seem unusual. Some states may require you to spend at least six months of the year in your domicile state.

- **Check the plan network:** Preferred Provider Organizations (PPO) plans are preferable to Exclusive Provider Organizations (EPO) and Health Maintenance Organizations (HMO) plans. If you're traveling outside of your home state, several EPO and HMO policies offer PPO-like benefits. However, in general, search for PPOs that will cover you across the country. If, on the other hand, you do not intend to travel for a year and will remain in your home state, you may not be concerned with nationwide coverage.

Recommended Plans:

Catastrophic, Bronze, Silver, Gold, and Platinum are the full-time RV medical insurance plans available under the Affordable Care Act.

If you're under 30, RVer Insurance Exchange recommends the Catastrophic plan because it's the lowest and qualifies you for coverage. This can be a solid bet because you're unlikely to use it at an early age (especially if you don't participate in any extreme activities).

If you're above the age of 30, a Bronze plan is recommended (or Silver, if you qualify for a subsidy to bring the cost down). The out-of-pocket maximum for Bronze plans is $6350 per person or $12,700 per family. Deductibles range from $1250 to $6350, but once you've met your deductible, you're covered 100% for covered medical and prescription medicines. Catastrophic, Bronze, Silver, Gold, and Platinum are the full-time RV medical insurance plans available under the Affordable Care Act.

If you're under 30, RVer Insurance Exchange recommends the Catastrophic plan because it's the lowest and qualifies you for coverage. This can be a solid bet because you're unlikely to use it at an early age (especially if you don't participate in any extreme activities).

If you're above the age of 30, a Bronze plan is recommended (or Silver, if you qualify for a subsidy to bring the cost down). The out-of-pocket maximum for Bronze plans is $6350 per person or $12,700 per family. Deductibles range from $1250 to $6350, but once you've met your deductible, you're covered 100% for covered medical and prescription medicines.

Telemedicine

Another alternative for full-time RVers is telemedicine. It's also a wonderful alternative when in-person medical appointments are required to be kept to a minimum. Telemedicine can be a terrific and economical solution when you don't need to be physically present at a doctor's office.

Telehealth can be used for a variety of purposes, from getting a prescription filled to getting a second opinion on lab results. You can also use them to figure out whether you need to go to urgent care or the ER.

Many of these businesses cater particularly to RVers, so they're already familiar with your situation and requirements. These services are available for a nominal monthly price and are well worth investigating, particularly if you value the peace of mind that comes with having immediate access to a skilled physician.

They're not a replacement for health insurance, but they're a good supplement if you just have catastrophic coverage and would have to pay for an office visit out of cash.

Medicare

If you're 65 or older, you're eligible for Medicare (a federal health insurance program). If you get Social Security Disability Insurance, you may also be eligible. If you think you could qualify, go to the Medicare website for further information.

Self-Employed Group Coverage

Look at Self-Employed Group Plans if you're self-employed but your income is too high to qualify for an ACA subsidy.

If you're the lone owner and employee of your company, you'll need to conduct some research to see if your state considers an individual to be a "group." If you manage a business with your partner, you may want to double-check if two or more people are considered a group.

The list of group coverage options is very similar to the list of individual coverage options, but in some circumstances, reduced rates are available.

Health Sharing

Another alternative is to use a Health Sharing service, which some RVers prefer. Many of these businesses are faith-based, and they seek sponsorship from a church in order to join.

It's vital to keep in mind that this isn't true health coverage. You are guaranteed coverage for any unforeseen medical bills in exchange for monthly dues. Members of the health share contribute to a pooled fund from which they can draw when they need it. Typically, any medical bills must be paid in full up ahead. The assumption is that you will be reimbursed by the health share after the fact (though this is not always guaranteed).

Supplemental Fixed Indemnity Plan

A Supplemental Fixed Indemnity Plan isn't exactly insurance, however. This is a refund plan that works on a case-by-case basis.

For example, if you dislocated your shoulder and needed surgery, you might obtain coverage that would pay you a set amount. The money would go to you, the policyholder, rather than the supplier. As a result, it's frequently utilized in conjunction with other types of insurance, particularly if you only have catastrophic coverage. However, because of the low cost, some people utilize this as their only source of insurance.

So what is the best medical insurance for full time RVers?

After some trial and error, we've decided that the short-term medical coverage we have today is the best option for us. Everyone is different when it comes to RV health insurance. When it comes to health care, we all have varied needs and risk tolerances. Examine the several full-time RVer health insurance alternatives and determine which one is best for you and your requirements. The available healthcare insurance for RVers vary every year, as we've observed personally. Before making a selection, do your homework and revisit your options at least once a year.

Summary

It may seem difficult to find RV health insurance on your own, but RVers have a variety of insurance options. We understand that sorting through them can be a pain, so we've tried to compile all of the information we've found most useful into one place.

The Right Type of Internet Connection

Traveling in an RV is a thrilling experience. You have the ability to go wherever you want, but it usually comes with a price - limited internet connectivity. Although great Internet is simple to come by when living close to large cities, finding a stable connection in the middle of nowhere is far more difficult. The good news is that there are numerous ways to connect to the internet while traveling by RV. We look at the most popular methods for staying connected, productive, and entertained when traveling in an RV in this post.

DSL & Cable Internet Access for RVs

The dial-up modem was about the only means for RVers to access the internet before the arrival of contemporary technology. At least one connection was available at several campgrounds and RV parks. However, traveling to the cable or DSL modem location, standing in line, or being cut off to allow others time were all major drawbacks.

DSL or cable internet connections have come a long way in recent years. It's becoming a popular choice for both homes and recreational vehicles. Unfortunately, on the road, a DSL or cable connection isn't a practical option for internet access. It only permits you to complete tasks online at a specific time before heading out to explore. Aside from that, its speeds are somewhat modest. As a result, in today's web-based world, dial-up connections do not satisfy the expectations of most RV travelers.

In some circumstances, the location of your camp may be beneficial. You might get DSL (if there are phone lines at the site) or cable service for your RV if you plan to stay in the same place for an extended period of time. Here are some suggestions to assist you:

PROVIDER	PRICE	PACKAGE	SPEEDS
AT&T	$49.99/mo.	DSL Package	10-100 Mbps
Frontier	$27.99/mo.	Frontier Internet	6 Mbps

Xfinity	$34.99/mo.	Performance Select	100 Mbps
CenturyLink	$49.99/mo.	Price for Life plan	100 Mbps

Wireless (Cellular) RV Internet Access

These days, cellular is by far the greatest way to stay connected when traveling. It's simple to put up, inexpensive, and quick (sometimes even faster than cable modems). You can establish a mobile hotspot and connect several devices with simply a smartphone or MIFI. To make the most of this option, pick a mobile network carrier with the most extensive coverage and the most affordable monthly pricing. The following are some of the most well-known cellphone internet providers:

- **Verizon** – is the most reputable cellular company with most coverage across the country.

- **AT&T** – is the second largest mobile network operator and covers a large part of the country. But, its LTE speeds aren't that high.

- **T-Mobile** – is the best choice for someone who wants a fast Internet. They have the best speeds, but less coverage than Verizon and AT&T

- **Sprint** – mainly provides service in cities and along interstates

Although mobile service is an excellent alternative for anyone who need high-speed internet, it is not without its drawbacks. Monthly or annual service contracts, for example, or having bandwidth throttled to lesser rates after exceeding defined limitations are examples of these. Another big issue is the lack of service coverage. To combat this, consider purchasing a 3G/4G cellular booster to improve the signal. If you have multiple phones, switching wireless service providers for each one may provide better service.

Satellite RV Internet Access

If you want to stay connected while you're out in the middle of nothing, satellite is the way to go. Satellite Internet is accessible from anyplace since signals are broadcast from space. All you need to do is make sure you have a clear view of the southern sky. Even better, most suppliers include VoIP phone service as well as TV signals. However, these added functionalities may necessitate the purchase of additional hardware. Typical satellite service providers include:

- HughesNet/Direcway

- Skyway
- Wildblue
- DISH
- DIRECTV
- Viasat

Satellite internet is great for high-volume consumption circumstances while on the go, but it's not for the faint of heart. It's possible that you'll spend around $1,300 only on the basic hardware. Depending on the satellite you're using, it might be even higher. Monthly plans for such equipment begin at $60 and go higher from there. Other disadvantages of the satellite include:

- Heavier hardware compared to other solutions.
- Restrictive fair access policies (FAP) that lower your speed if you exceed the daily, weekly, or monthly limits.
- Decreased speeds during peak hours, usually 4 to 10 p.m.
- Inclement weather (fog, snow, or rain) may also degrade the service.
- Unreliable latency especially if you need gaming, streaming media, or Voice-over-IP (VoIP) services.
- Requires a certain level of technical know-how and troubleshooting ability should connectivity problems arise in the wilderness.

Free WiFi RV Internet Access

You can always use free WiFi if you aren't too concerned about remaining connected or don't want to spend any money on the Internet. Wireless hotspots can now be found in practically every location. There's a good chance the campsite or RV park where you're staying has one. The benefit of free WiFi is that it eliminates the need for cables or other clumsy infrastructure. To get online in the comfort of your RV, all you need is a computer or other device with a WiFi card or adapter.

While a wireless hotspot is an excellent temporary solution, it does have certain drawbacks. Free WiFi isn't always assured, especially if you're on the road. You have no control over how distant your RV is from the router or how good the network is if there is one. The majority of campers' WiFi networks aren't very good. It's also possible that the site will be overloaded. As a result, you may need to invest in WiFi extender equipment, such as a WiFi Range Extender.

What is the Best Internet Services Option?

Simply said, the greatest internet service is a balance of benefits and drawbacks. In other words, the optimum option will be determined by your specific needs and budget. Cellular networks, for example, are ideal for users who require high-speed internet and must be able to stay connected in nearly any location. On the other hand, satellite internet is great for tourists who venture too far off the usual path and frequently lack mobile connection. If you really must stay connected while on the road, a combination of the two may provide you with acceptable RV internet service.
Whatever method you use, make sure to take all necessary security procedures to safeguard your device and personal data.

The Right Type of GPS

Remember when you had to carry a paper map or atlas with you wherever you went? You'd plan your itinerary before leaving home and stop to double-check that you were on the proper road. Then there were websites like MapQuest, which let you plan your trip and print detailed directions. We now have all of that and more in the palm of our hands, due to cellphones and RV GPS gadgets!
Listen up if you're seeking for the greatest RV GPS. Here are some of the greatest devices, apps, and strategies for putting these helpful hints into practice.

Best RV GPS:

1. Garmin RV 785 GPS Navigator
2. Rand McNally OverDryve 7 RV GPS
3. Garmin RV 770 LMT-S GPS Navigator
4. TomTom Trucker 620

What Makes an RV GPS Special?

"Why do I need a particular GPS for my RV?" you might think. Isn't it possible for me to use the one I have for my car?"
You can, but you'll be losing out on several key features that will greatly assist RV drivers on the road. Aside from the obvious navigation ability, there are a few advantages:

- Avoiding low bridges
- Taking your rig's weight into consideration
- Avoiding narrow roads

Driving a huge vehicle, such as an RV, is not the same as driving a car, therefore don't use the same GPS. Of course, you don't want just any unit — you want the best of the best, one that will safely transport you from one location to the next!

Best RV GPS Units

There are a lot of GPSs to select from, happily (or unfortunately, if you're indecisive). Here are four of the best GPS systems on the market right now.

1. Garmin RV 785 GPS Navigator

This device will provide bespoke routing based on the size and weight of your setup. Road warnings for steep hills and sharp curves are included, as well as a list of RV parks and amenities and smartphone Bluetooth connectivity. This model also includes a dash cam that records your drive and saves film automatically if an issue is detected.
Display size: 7"
Price: $399.99 on Amazon.com

2. Rand McNally OverDryve 7 RV GPS

This GPS unit has award-winning RV navigation, hands-free phone and text calling, and a trip planner with the Tripmaker software built in. The OverDryve, like the Garmin 785, has a dashcam that records the road (and any possible accidents) ahead of you.
Display size: 7"
Price: $399 on Amazon

3. Garmin RV 770 LMT-S GPS Navigator

This Garmin also creates unique routes based on the size and weight of the RV or trailer being towed. Bluetooth calling, smart notifications, and voice-activated navigation are just a few of the hands-free capabilities included. You can also get free access to live traffic, basic weather, and more if you download the free Smartphone Link app to your smartphone. With built-in WiFi, you can update maps and software without needing to use a computer.
Display size: 6.95"
Price: $299 on Amazon

4. TomTom Trucker 620

You can navigate the roads like a trucker with a lifetime supply of truck maps and TomTom traffic. The "My Vehicle" function lets you to enter the length, width, height, and weight of your vehicle to determine the best route for you.
Display size: 6" (also comes in a smaller 5" screen)
Price: $255 on Amazon

Best Smartphone Apps for RV Navigation

Nowadays, your phone can perform all of these functions. Check out these four apps if you want to save money and utilize your smartphone as a GPS.

- **CoPilot GPS Navigation**

Many people rely on this software, particularly truck drivers and RVers, because of its unique RV navigation features. You can stay on the finest routes and stay away from low bridges and truck-only lanes. Routes will be tailored to your RV's size, and you'll be able to search through millions of pre-loaded destinations, such as campgrounds and rest spots.
Price: Free

- **InRoute Route Planner**

Although this isn't a navigation program, it is a useful tool for organizing road trips. This software lets you construct personalized routes depending on weather, elevation, road curviness, and other factors. You can even create your own itinerary, adding up to 150 stops leg per leg. If you're worried about the weather while driving, InRoute can help. You may even sync your routes to other apps for step-by-step navigation, such as Google Maps.
Price: $3.99/mo or $29.99/year

- **Google Maps and Waze**

These two navigation apps are often used by the average driver. They're fantastic for regular car use, but they don't have any unique features for RV drivers. Still, if you have a tiny enough rig, they might be ideal for your journeys!
Price: Free

Tips for Using Your GPS in Your RV

Improper GPS use can result in inattentive driving, which can lead to accidents. When using your GPS on the road, always keep these helpful hints in mind.

- Never fully rely on your GPS:It's usually a good idea to have some notion of how to get to your goal, even if it's just knowing where you're supposed to go. In the event that the device fails, it is also beneficial to download offline maps or carry a paper map or atlas.

- Pre-enter your destination. Don't put off fiddling with the GPS until you're on the road. Always do this before getting on the road to keep your hands free.

- Let your passenger help you:Allow your passenger to adjust your path if you need to while you're on the road. If you're alone, pull over to a safe location, such as a parking lot, to make the necessary adjustments.

- Mount your GPS where it is visible but not in the way of your view. It's easier to keep your eyes on the road when it's mounted.

However, before you mount that GPS, double-check that it's legal where you are and where you intend to go. In some states, mounting your GPS is really prohibited.

Where It's Illegal to Use a GPS

Some states have legislation prohibiting the use of GPS systems or smartphones mounted on the windshield. The laws for each state are listed below.

- Alabama: Suction cup attachments on the windshield are prohibited; GPS must be placed elsewhere.

- Alaska: Suction cup mounts on the windshield are permissible as long as they are not in the driver's direct line of sight.

- Arizona: Windshield mounts are permitted at the lowest 5" of the driver's side and the bottom 7" of the passenger's side.

- Arkansas: In the 4.5" above the bottom of the windshield, windshield mounts are permitted.

- California: Windshield mounts are allowed in the bottom 5" of the driver's side or bottom 7" of the passenger side of the windshield.

- Colorado: Windshield suction cup mounts are illegal; GPS must be mounted elsewhere.

- Connecticut: Windshield suction cup mounts are illegal; GPS must be mounted elsewhere.

- Delaware: Windshield suction cup mounts are illegal; GPS must be mounted elsewhere.

- Florida: Specific devices (GPS devices ONLY) may be mounted; the driver's view cannot be obstructed.

- Georgia: Windshield suction cup mounts are legal as long as they aren't mounted in the driver's direct line of sight.

- Hawaii: Windshield mounts are allowed in the bottom 5" of the driver's side or bottom 7" of the passenger side of the windshield.

- Idaho: Windshield suction cup mounts are illegal; GPS must be mounted elsewhere.

- Illinois: Windshield suction cup mounts are illegal; GPS must be mounted elsewhere.

- Indiana: Windshield mounts are allowed in the bottom 4" of the passenger side.

- Iowa: Windshield suction cup mounts are legal as long as they aren't mounted in the driver's direct line of sight.

- Kansas: Windshield suction cup mounts are legal as long as they aren't mounted in the driver's direct line of sight.

- Kentucky: Windshield suction cup mounts are legal as long as they aren't mounted in the driver's direct line of sight.

- Louisiana: Windshield suction cup mounts are illegal; GPS must be mounted elsewhere.

- Maine: Windshield suction cup mounts are illegal; GPS must be mounted elsewhere.

- Maryland: Windshield mounts are allowed in the bottom 7" of the passenger side.

- Massachusetts: Windshield suction cup mounts are legal as long as they aren't mounted in the driver's direct line of sight.

- Michigan: Device can be mounted, but devices are limited to ones for navigation, traffic, weather conditions, vehicle conditions, or road conditions.

- Minnesota: Specific devices (GPS devices ONLY) may be mounted on the bottom part of the windshield; the driver's view cannot be obstructed.

- Mississippi: Windshield suction cup mounts are legal as long as they aren't mounted in the driver's direct line of sight.

- Missouri: Windshield suction cup mounts are legal as long as they aren't mounted in the driver's direct line of sight.

- Montana: Windshield suction cup mounts are illegal; GPS must be mounted elsewhere.

- Nebraska: Windshield suction cup mounts are illegal; GPS must be mounted elsewhere.

- Nevada: Windshield suction cup mounts are legal as long as they aren't mounted in the driver's direct line of sight.

- New Hampshire: Device can be mounted, but devices are limited to ones for navigation, traffic, weather conditions, vehicle conditions, or road conditions.

- New Jersey: Windshield suction cup mounts are illegal; GPS must be mounted elsewhere.

- New Mexico: Windshield suction cup mounts are illegal; GPS must be mounted elsewhere.

- New York: Windshield suction cup mounts are illegal; GPS must be mounted elsewhere.

- North Carolina: Device can be mounted, but devices are limited to ones for navigation, traffic, weather conditions, vehicle conditions, or road conditions.

- North Dakota: Windshield suction cup mounts are illegal; GPS must be mounted elsewhere.

- Ohio: Windshield suction cup mounts are legal as long as they aren't mounted in the driver's direct line of sight.

- Oklahoma: Windshield suction cup mounts are illegal; GPS must be mounted elsewhere.

- Oregon: Windshield suction cup mounts are illegal; GPS must be mounted elsewhere.

- Pennsylvania: Windshield suction cup mounts are legal as long as they aren't mounted in the driver's direct line of sight.

- Rhode Island: Windshield suction cup mounts are legal as long as they aren't mounted in the driver's direct line of sight.

- South Carolina: Windshield suction cup mounts are legal as long as they aren't mounted in the driver's direct line of sight.

- South Dakota: Windshield suction cup mounts are legal as long as they aren't mounted in the driver's direct line of sight.

- Tennessee: Windshield suction cup mounts are legal as long as they aren't mounted in the driver's direct line of sight.

- Texas: Windshield suction cup mounts are legal as long as they aren't mounted in the driver's direct line of sight.

- Utah: Windshield mounts are allowed in the top 4" of the whole windshield or the bottom 4" of the driver side of the windshield.

- Vermont: Windshield mounts are allowed in the bottom 4" of the passenger side of the windshield.

- Virginia: Windshield suction cup mounts are illegal; GPS must be mounted elsewhere.

- Washington: Windshield suction cup mounts are illegal; GPS must be mounted elsewhere.

- West Virginia: Windshield suction cup mounts are illegal; GPS must be mounted elsewhere.

- Wisconsin: Device can be mounted, but devices are limited to ones for navigation, traffic, weather conditions, vehicle conditions, or road conditions.

- Wyoming: Windshield mounts are allowed anywhere above the AS-1 tint line.

Remember that most states have a distracted driving rule that only allows these gadgets to be used while driving if they are hands-free. If you're driving, don't try to use a GPS.

Navigate the Open Road

Now that you know where you're heading, it's time to take your RV out on the open road. Pack your belongings, enter your location, and go on an adventure!

Storage and Space-Saving Tips

You can always need additional storage space in your RV, whether you have a 40' diesel pusher or a 20' teardrop camper. These RV storage tricks and techniques can help you get the most out of your RV cabinets, worktops, and outside storage sections.

Kitchen

When it comes to clutter, the kitchen is a significant headache. Most campers can always benefit from additional kitchen space.

- For dry foods like rice, pasta, and cereal, invest in square jars. They can be stacked and arranged closely on a shelf.

- Instead of buying a full-sized blender, look for smaller versions of larger machines. Installing an under cabinet mounted coffee pot can help save up counter space.

- Use the insides of cabinet doors as a source of inspiration. Small plastic shelves can be hung to hold light items like plastic wrap and foil. Pot and pan lids can also be hung within cabinet doors.

- Do you enjoy cooking with spices? To make greater use of cupboard space, use strong magnet strips to stick metal storage cans stocked with herbs and spices in out-of-the-way places.

Living Area

Make the most of your living space. You'll be surprised at how much extra space you can make by organizing your RV effectively.

- Be inventive! For flashlights, broom holder clips work well, and velcro keeps remote controls safely out of the way.

- Fragile things can be wrapped in extra throw blankets while in transit.

- To save space, discard the board game boxes and place all of the pieces and cards in sandwich baggies.

Bathroom

Many RV bathrooms have limited cabinet space and might benefit greatly from space-saving techniques.

- Cut pieces of PVC pipe and attach them on the inside of cabinet doors. Curling iron and cord are neatly tucked away and out of the way.

- Use elastic mounted in loops along the back of your medicine cabinet to keep tubes of cream standing upright rather than lying down. This allows you to make more room on your shelf.

- Take smaller amounts of shampoo and mouthwash from larger bottles for short travels. Wire or hooks can be used to suspend small bottles from the shower curtain pole.

Bedroom

Long RV journeys necessitate innovative storage solutions for your full vacation clothing.

- For convenient sock, belt, and shoe pockets, cut a hanging cloth shoe holder into rows and install them on the side of the bed.

- Out-of-season clothing should be packed and stored in an exterior container or under the bed.

- Create a storage headboard for books, cell phones, glasses, and other items by suspending fabric compartments from a decorative curtain rod.

Outside

There are a variety of ways to make the most of your outside compartments.

- Purchase storage containers. You can stack objects and make the most of your vertical space by using multiple plastic containers with lids.

- Clips from the top of the storage compartment or the compartment door can be used to hang brooms and other uncomfortable things.

- Slide out trays allow you to make the most of your storage space while also making it easier to grab items.

- The Heartland Trail Runner, for example, has a rear storage rack. This is the ideal location for moving large items such as bicycles and coolers.

Gadgets

Is there anything better than a recreational vehicle? Of course, a rig that's well-equipped with the latest RV technology! Having the correct equipment on board can make your vacation much more convenient and enjoyable. It's all about locating the accessories that make day-to-day living on the road a little easier.

RV gadgets and gizmos may assist you with every aspect of your camping trip, from making it easier to decorate your RV to preparing a memorable gourmet dinner in your onboard kitchen. We've also included RV gadgets that make cleaning your travel trailer or motorhome a pleasure rather than a burden, as well as RV gadgets that make your rig a safer travel environment.

Having the correct gear along for the voyage, whether it's your own rig or not, may make a significant difference. So, if you're ready to take your next vacation to the next level, keep reading. The greatest RV camping devices and accessories that you must have on board are listed below.

- Quake Hold: If you're anything like me, you want to personalize your computer and make it feel like a home. You can safely exhibit your favorite dinnerware, rock collection, or tchotchkes with Quake Hold. Any hard surface can be secured with a small amount of Quake Hold putty under your item. Simply twist it when you're ready to move it. When traveling, the object will stay put, but when you try to move it, it will come off.

- Command Strips: A RVer's best buddy is Command Strips. Command Strips will fasten your object to the RV wall without damaging it, whether you want to display photos, paintings, or a mirror. Do you need to relocate something? It's no problem. Simply lift the tab to detach the strip from the wall.

- Command Hooks: Hooks are also available under the Command brand. These hooks are available in a variety of forms and sizes. You can use them to hang your purse, coat, or keys. You may even have shower hooks that are water resistant. It's fantastic!

- Vinyl Wall Art: Vinyl wall art in a range of colors and styles can be found in abundance on Etsy and Ebay. You may personalize your fridge, mirrors, cabinets, and walls with swirls, sayings, and other designs. Make it more enjoyable! Add some vinyl to the mix.

- Light Blocking Curtains: Curtains give a room texture and dimension. They also keep the heat out. Light-blocking drapes, which can be found at Walmart, Target, and Hobby Lobby, are an excellent addition to any RV. They will not only soften and modify your RV, but they will also save you money. The cost of heating and cooling adds up. Light-blocking curtains add more insulation to your home, lowering your utility expenditures. Isn't that appealing?

RV Kitchen Gadgets

The kitchen is the beating heart of any home, including mobile homes. Here are a few RV cooking gadgets that will leave you wanting more.

- Instant Pot: We've said it before, and we'll probably say it again. But, really, are you camping at all if you're not using an Instant Pot? The Instant Pot is our favorite culinary gadget for RVers since it can slow cook, pressure cook, sauté, steam, and even produce perfect rice and yogurt all with one small and reasonable footprint. In fact, we've created an entire piece about why you should buy one (and what to do with it once you do!).

- Slow Cooker Liners: Any RV would benefit from having a crock pot. They cook without a lot of heat being released. Life gets even easier with slow cooker liners. Fill your slow cooker with food and a slow cooker liner. Simply toss the liner when you've completed your supper, and your pot is clean!
- Reynolds Wrap: A camper's best friend is foil packets. Reynolds Wrap is ideal for constructing pillow-style meal packages that can be cooked over an open fire or on a grill. There is no cleanup and the portions are small. What's not to like about that?
- Toaster Oven: Your oven, if you're like many other RVers, is the kitchen equipment you miss the most from your stick-and-bricks house. The microwave's convection setting just isn't the same.
- A toaster oven, on the other hand, allows you to cook a variety of baked and toasted treats directly on your countertop, as well as quick and easy appetizers like quesadillas, English muffin pizzas, and more!

- Solar Oven: When you don't have to, why heat up your kitchen? Cook your food in the sun. The GoSun portable cooker is a cylinder-style oven that is simple to use. It's easy to store because it folds down. Another economical choice is the HotLogic Mini Personal Portable Oven oven, which is similar but requires you to plug it in!
- Cuisinart Smart Stick Immersion Blender: This baby is capable of chopping, blending, stirring, and whipping. Its small size makes it ideal for RVs.
- Stovetop Cover: If you're anything like me, you're always short on counter space. That's why I'm a big fan of the Camco cooktop cover. It fits over your burners to enlarge your kitchen counter area instantaneously, allowing you to cut, slice, chop, and prepare to your heart's (and stomach's) desire.
- Fridge Bars: While traveling, the Camco double refrigerator bar keeps food from shifting. My gallon jugs of milk and water are secured on the top shelf with mine. They only take 5 seconds to install and are a great buy at $5.

Cleaning RV Gadgets

It is critical to keep your rig clean for both your own health and the longevity of your rig. Cleaning, on the other hand, is a duty that few of us enjoy doing... However, having the correct tools and accessories can be quite beneficial! Here are a few things that will make cleaning your RV a little easier.

- Shower Squeegee:Moisture is the RV's worst enemy. A simple shower squeegee helps keep the moisture out of your shower. It will also assist in keeping your shower cleaner for longer. Squeegees are affordable and quite effective.
- RainX:Do you believe RainX is only for windshields? Reconsider your position. On glass shower doors, rain works wonders. The water from the shower will bead and roll off the glass. There are no stains. There's no mildew here!
- Collapsible Tub: Dishwashing tubs, foot baths, and general cleaning are all fantastic uses for collapsible tubs. When you're not using it, pop it up. It's best to put it away while it's not in use. That's all there is to it!
- Spray Bottle: Fill a spray bottle halfway with water and a drop of dish soap. Before you put your dishes in the sink, spray them. This easy process will act as a pre-soak, allowing you to use less water when it comes time to wash.

Laundry RV Gadgets

Laundry never stops, even when you're on vacation! Keeping your clothes clean, however, does not have to be a chore. It's a lot easier with these tools!

- Color Catchers: If you use the laundromat frequently, as many campers do, you'll like this device. Shout Color Catchers might assist you in saving money. Don't worry about sorting if you use a big washer. Combine all of your fabrics and add a color catcher. The color catcher catches any dye that tries to escape and keeps it away from your other garments. You can save a lot of money by washing and drying everything at the same time. WOW!
- Plastic Washing Bin: Traveling and don't have time to wash your socks and underwear? It's no problem. Fill a plastic bin halfway with cold water and a dash of soap. To ensure a secure fit, click the lid on. Put the bin in your shower and get ready to go. The movement of your rig will stir the garments at the conclusion of the day. Simply rinse and hang to dry. The ideal washer for an emergency!
- Over The Door Organizer: This may or may not apply to laundry, but it unquestionably does to organization. Makeup, shoes, and workplace necessities may all be kept in one place with a multi-pocket organizer. You may even cut the organizers in half and reuse them multiple times. Use command hooks to install them on the inside of cupboards or the base of your bed, or hang them on the back of a door. SO SIMPLE.

Safety RV Gadgets

While having a good time is crucial, safety should always come first, both on the road and at home. Don't leave home without these RV safety equipment, and make sure your emergency pack is up to date as well!

- Corner Guards: If you have a slide on your rig, you know how easy it is to hit your head. Those corners can be really painful, especially if you are directly beneath one. Corner guards provide a gentler edge and protect your head and arms from being cut. ARE YOU ABLE TO SAY IT WAS WORTH IT?
- Fire Extinguisher:This is a foregone conclusion. At all times, you should have at least two extinguishers on hand: one for the engine and one for the kitchen. Check to see if they're up to date and safe. You need to know it works in an emergency!

- Carbon Monoxide Alarm: Get a Carbon Monoxide Alarm if your vehicle didn't come with one. Gas leaks that humans can't always smell are detected by these devices. This is especially critical if you have a diesel pusher and your bed is next to the engine in the back. REMEMBER TO BE SAFE!
- Mini Paper Shredder: The security of your mail does not cease just because you are on vacation. For the full-time RVer, a tiny paper shredder is a must-have equipment. Choose a crosscut unit that will replicate your data while keeping it safe from criminals.
- Portable Dehumidifier: A dehumidifier is required if you reside in your RV all year. Moisture is an RV's worst enemy, and you'd be surprised how much moisture a vehicle can hold. To keep the air dry and avoid leaky skylights, I use a portable dehumidifier. Seavon produces a small model that can dehumidify up to 170 square feet, making it ideal for all but the largest travel trailers and motorhomes. My best piece of advice? Spend the money now to avoid having to pay for repairs later!

Electronic RV Gadgets

Just because you're not at home doesn't mean your preoccupation with technology has to end! These electrical RV devices are a must-have for making your rig a lot more futuristic.

- Cell Signal Booster: When your phone calls, you're camping in the middle of nowhere. You don't have enough bars to take the call, unfortunately. You dash left and right in a futile attempt to locate a signal. So, what are your options? Easy! A cell booster will extend your phone's range, especially inside an RV. There are a variety of units available, so read reviews to get the one that's right for you. Is it possible for you to hear me now?
- WiFi Booster: It's just a decent value if the free wifi works. Increase your chances by placing a wifi booster on top of your computer. For serious internet users, the WiFi Ranger with signal enhancer is a must-have. Sure, it won't fix your problematic connections, but it will improve your capacity to use the ones that are working.
- Solar Powered Cell Phone Charger: When you don't have to, why plug in? Solar phone chargers are an excellent method to conserve energy while remaining connected. Solar chargers for phones, tablets, and computers are available, and some even come with backpacks. Please add me to the list!

- Mighty Spotify Music Player: Remember when everyone had an iPod and a collection of MP3s to go with it? Many of us now use streaming music services such as Spotify to listen to music, but that doesn't mean you can't bring your carefully curated playlists with you.
- The Mighty Spotify Music Player allows you to take your music with you everywhere you go, without the need for a WiFi or data connection. It's Bluetooth-enabled and also works with wired headphones, so you can listen as you like.
- Bluetooth Speaker: Bluetooth is a friend in reverse. There are no wires required. A Bluetooth speaker may connect to a wide range of electronic devices. Experiment with extra amplitude on your phone, television, iPad, iPod, or even your radio. Take the sound with you and make your life a lot easier!
- The Oontz Angle 3 also comes with the extra benefit of being water proof, so you can jam in the shower or outside in the rain. It also comes in a variety of colors and can charge for up to 14 hours!
- Roku:If your RV park has good WiFi, you can use a Roku to watch hundreds of on-demand TV channels (many of which are free!) You may also access Netflix, Hulu, Crackle, and a number of other streaming services. When you have a Roku, who needs satellite?
- Fans:With or without air conditioning, small, portable fans are crucial for keeping your equipment cool. Air movement improves the efficiency of your air conditioner. It also keeps things inside fresh. Because any RV must be compact and multifunctional, I recommend the Honeywell Turbo Force Fan. These units can be found almost anywhere. They are low-cost, strong, and silent, and they can be utilized for a range of tasks. They can be used to keep clothes cool and dry or to drive hot air out the windows.

Miscellaneous Must Have RV Gadgets

Here are a few more gadgets and gizmos that defy category yet can significantly improve your camping experience!

- The Electric Fly Swatter: Yup. They're made, and some RVers can't imagine living without them. Electric fly swatters or bug fryers are an excellent way to keep pests out of your RV.

- Fire Pit: Enclosed fire pits are permissible in many national and private parks, and they give your campsite a cozy vibe at night. If you enjoy fire, consider purchasing a portable device or building your own.

Portable Solar Panels: Solar panels are all the rage, but if you don't want to permanently place them on your rig, there are still options. 120W solar kits with a 10 amp controller are available from Go Power! These units are foldable for storage and may be set up anywhere. They come with a carrying case and 15 feet of cable. What can solar power do for you? When you're not plugged in, these panels will keep your battery charged. This translates to hours of extra enjoyment in your RV when wild camping.

Chapter 5: Full-Time Rv-ing with Family

What is Workamping

Workamping is work in exchange for a camping site (and generally payment) in a campground or RV resort for a set period of time, usually during the high to shoulder season. Work might be part-time or full-time, for a couple or an individual. Positions are typically for a couple with their own RV. The remuneration can include any of the following:

- Paid hours
- A free or discounted RV campground with hookups and some amenities like laundry and Wifi.
- You'll get paid hours and a free or discounted spot for your RV.

Workamping assignments might range from full-time jobs for both partners to part-time jobs for one or both. Workampers may be paid an hourly wage or may not be paid at all, receiving only a free website in exchange for their time. The combinations are extremely changeable and should be thoroughly described ahead of time.

How to Assess a Job Offer for Workamping

To see if the job is a good value, multiply the number of hours necessary by the current hourly rate (or minimum wage) in the area. Compare that figure to the going fee for the campground you've been assigned.

For example:

For a free site with no paid hours, a couple must put in 40 hours per week. If the local minimum wage is $8.00, 40 hours would be worth $320 per week, or about $1300 per month. If a campsite can be rented for $1000 per month, it's a horrible deal for a workamper because you're earning less than minimum wage. However, in some circumstances, you cannot stay in a park for more than 30 days per season, so if you truly want to be there, the contract may be more appealing.

Be Sure to Read Your Work Camping Contract Carefully

There are some businesses that aim to take advantage of RVers. For example, in the case above, by offering nothing but a free site for practically full-time work. Or by proposing a seasonal rate that, after doing the calculation, turns out to be less than the minimum wage. Before you sign on, always request a contract and read it thoroughly.

You don't have to accept a lousy job because there are lots of reliable employers out there. Slaves were given board and food during the dreadful age of slavery. So, if you agree to work for nothing but an RV park, you are effectively working as a slave!

How to Find Workamping Jobs

There are several websites that post job openings in the United States, as well as one or two that list job openings in Canada (see below). You can also use services like Indeed to look for job openings. Setting up a job alert so that you are notified by email when new postings are posted is a good idea wherever you browse.

You can expect to find listings anywhere from three to eleven months before the start date. During September and October, we began receiving job alerts for spring opportunities in Arizona.

In Canada, Parks Canada may begin advertising as early as November, while other businesses often begin their search for summer seasonal work after Christmas. When we stay at locations where we think we could love working, we also inquire. This allows us to do an in-person interview, which may increase your chances of being chosen.

Useful Web Sites to Find Workamping Opportunities

https://www.workamper.com/

This one isn't free, but the Intro is, and it's a very professional and highly recommended site with a wealth of information.

https://www.happyvagabonds.com

This is a free site where we found a summer employment.

https://workingcouples.com/jobs-category/work-campers-campground

Companies seeking for work campers can discover you on this free site, which allows you to search for jobs by region and kind. You can even add your CV to help employers find you.

https://www.work-for-rvers-and-campers.com/help-wanted.html

Helpful site for free Advertisements for work campers, as well as a variety of other resources. It's just a list; there's no way to search inside places, for instance.

http://workampingjobs.com/

Help Wanted ads are available for free on this site. It only contains a job listing; there is no possibility to search by location.

Duties of a Workamper

Workampers usually sign an agreement that will outline the duties, pay, minimum hours, and any other conditions of employment. The agreement may also include protections, such as workers' compensation regulations in the event of injury. The duties one performs as a work camper can include:

- Grounds cleaning – Raking the lawn, cleaning the fire pit, returning unneeded fuel, and so on

- Facilities maintenance – Cleaning toilets or outhouses, emptying garbage and recycling bins, and maintaining the lawn or ground cover

- Administrative duties – Reservations, check-in and check-out of visitors, and sales are all handled over the phone.

- Hospitality – Greeting visitors, answering questions, and enforcing park policies and safety procedures with compassion.

- Social activities – Hikes, nature walks, card games, fitness exercises, and other group activities for guests

- Commerce – Customers are served at an on-site store.

- Camp hosting – Staying on a job site throughout the entire season to meet and assist visitors.

Taxation Issues for Work Campers

Although not all employers provide tax receipts to workampers, it is becoming more commonplace. Some employers will factor in the value of the free or low-cost camping in their salary calculations. You should be aware of your employer's policies ahead of time so that you can plan how to declare your earnings and pay your taxes.

You may be eligible to deduct some or all of the costs of uniforms and/or transport to and from the worksite, depending on the tax legislation in your home province or state. To make these deductions, you may need to obtain a declaration or taxes form from your employer.

Workamping Outside of Your Own Country

When recruiting work campers, some employers do not inquire about citizenship, especially if the firm does not offer tax documentation. This practice, however, is dwindling, and more firms are treating work campers like any other employee.
If you are a Canadian working in the United States or a US citizen working in Canada, keep in mind that you may be working illegally. If this is uncovered, you may face a lengthy ban from visiting to that nation. It is not, in our opinion, worth the risk.

Is Workamping for You?

Workampers must be even-tempered, flexible, and diplomatic in order to be successful. It's also necessary to be able to strike a balance between safety standards and rules and consideration for guest experiences. This necessitates a high level of common sense and judgment. Workamping can be a physically difficult work, so being in good physical condition is normally required.

A Few Words of Caution about Workamping

If you've spent your entire career in management, finding yourself scrubbing toilets can be jarring. Also, you'll probably find yourself getting commands from the same folks who used to give you orders! This is due to the fact that many park managers have little or no professional management training. As a result, you must be willing to leave your ego at the door and accept commands, even if you disagree with them.

I went from being a senior manager leading a huge firm with global responsibilities to following orders from someone who had no management training at all in one of my workamping positions (which I will NOT name). For some reason, she assumed that everyone who worked for her was completely inept. We had to sit down and talk about it, and things were better after that. I kept my ego in check and listened to her leadership suggestions. But, rather than being treated like an inexperienced adolescent, I insisted on being handled with respect.

So, as a new work camper, your role is to be a part of the team and follow instructions. You should, however, demand that you be treated fairly, that you are given proper training, and that you are safeguarded by good safety standards. If you are not safe, you should leave the job as soon as possible. It's simply not worth it to be wounded on the job. Also, look at the contract to see if there is any form of worker protection.

Other Considerations Before You Accept an Offer for a Work Camping Job

Because you are usually committed for a whole season, you want to be sure you will be satisfied with the position! Make sure you receive a complete list of tasks and consider whether you are a suitable fit. For example, if you despise meeting new people, you will not enjoy working in a crowded workplace seeing new visitors every day.

Gender-Based Expectations in Workamping

It's worth noting that most positions for male camp employees need all-day physical exertion as well as a variety of handyman abilities. If you've spent your entire working life in an office, you can be exhausted, or you might just lack the necessary abilities. Joe was completely taken aback by his first workamping experience. He was suddenly expected to have all kinds of handyman abilities that he simply did not have after 30 years of dealing with computers. Thanks to a supporting team, he was able to get by. However, now that Joe is aware of the high expectations placed on male camp workers, he believes he should have been more forthright about his limits before accepting the job. As a result, the employer would have the option of providing training or hiring someone else. He was well aware during the season that he had fallen short of expectations, which was difficult for him to accept.

If you're a female work camper, on the other hand, you'll be required to be polite, helpful, and hospitable, as well as have a variety of computer and customer-service abilities. Because you will almost definitely be working in the check-in office, this is the case. Workamping will be challenging for you if this profile does not fit you.

Sexism in Workamping

That reminds me of another element of working at a campground: most campgrounds are extremely sexist in their hiring practices. Men are expected to labor on the grounds, while women are expected to work in the office. In this day and age, we find this to be quite remarkable. Joe has exceptional people and computer abilities, but he is not welcome in the office because he is a man. I'm a strong woman with outstanding handyman skills, but I'm not normally sought on a grounds crew because I'm a woman. It's bizarre.

In summary, if you and your spouse don't quite fit gender expectations, workamping may be problematic. You will also have a hard time finding a couple employment if you are not a married, heterosexual pair. Regardless of your ability to complete the task. We know a female couple who would love to work at a campground, but we had to tell them that most campgrounds are unlikely to recruit them. It's shocking, sad, and unfair... yet it's true.

Workamping F.A.Q

What is Workamping?

There are some misunderstandings regarding who Workampers are and what Workamping entails. The most popular misconceptions about Workampers are that they are retirees who work at campgrounds and that Workamping simply entails exchanging work for a space to park an RV.

To begin with, Workampers are not all retired. In fact, just around half of Workampers consider themselves to be retired. With a typical age of 53, it's clear that the bulk of Workampers aren't on a fixed income and can't live off of rent-free camping alone. Workamping, on the other hand, refers to any activity that involves exchanging man/woman hours for something of value.

While the term Workamper does not appear in Webster's dictionary, it does appear in the United States Patent and Trademark Office. The following is the official definition: Workampers are adventurous individuals and couples who have chosen to combine any type of part-time or full-time job with RV camping. Our registered trademark "WorkCamper" with a "C" is just another way of spelling this unique name.

There is no mention of "retirement" or "campgrounds" in the definition. You are a Workamper if you eat and sleep in an RV and engage in any activity in exchange for something of value. While this description might theoretically cover occupations as diverse as construction laborers and race car drivers, Dale Earnhardt, Jr. is unlikely to be referred to as a Workamper! When we use the term "workamper," we're referring to those whose primary occupation is in the outdoor hospitality business.

Who are Workampers?

Workampers are people of all ages and backgrounds who work on a variety of projects while traveling in their RVs. (Some firms offer lodging to employees who do not own an RV.) Some Workampers are full-time RVers, while others are part-timers. Some work for government agencies and non-profits, while the majority work for businesses of all sorts, from small "mom and pop" shops to large enterprises. Many labor for a certain amount of hours in exchange for a site, hookups, and other amenities, while others are paid hourly or on a salary basis. Some people work for both the site and the pay.

Some Workampers run their own companies. Some people work part-time, while others work full-time. Some people work seasonally, whereas others work all year. Some people Workamp because they enjoy being active and productive, while others are motivated by the money and benefits. Workamping is viewed by some as a one-time adventure, while others see it as an exciting new way of life—either way, they can choose from thousands of amazing jobs in fantastic locations!

What is the number one advantage of the Workamper Lifestyle?

Freedom of Place: Because of your Workamper income and advantages, you can go wherever you choose and stay as long as you want.

For example, it takes months to thoroughly explore Yellowstone Park, although the average visit lasts only a few days due to the high expense of living and campground stay limits. Workaholics who spend the entire summer in Yellowstone get to know the park like locals! Warm winters, cool summers, time with the grandkids, time away from the grandkids, and a million other tantalizing benefits are all part of the Freedom of Place package!

What kinds of positions are available?

It's all up to you! As fresh and intriguing opportunities come in from a variety of organizations, the answer to this question varies on a daily basis. Camp hosts, park managers, activities directors, grounds keepers, maintenance workers, caretakers, and site-sitters are some of the more prevalent positions.

Artists, musicians, tram and shuttle bus drivers, RV delivery drivers, field reps, cooks, tour guides, park rangers, sales workers, RV technicians, and utilities inspectors are among the positions that have been advertised. We also have opportunities in theme parks, canoe/kayak outfitters, golf courses, motorsports venues, circuses/carnivals, hunting & fishing camps, guest ranches, marinas, museums, gift shops, lodges, ski resorts, wildlife refuges, and youth camps on a regular basis. Actors for wild west shows, tail-gunners for RV caravans, chuckwagon cooks, pumpkin lot and Christmas tree lot managers, and a variety of other unusual occupations are occasionally needed.

How much do these jobs pay?

The pay scales are as diverse as the jobs themselves. For many part-time occupations, it can range from an RV site or housing exchange—including utilities—to competitive pay plus health insurance, retirement, and other benefits for full-time career work. Employers of temporary or seasonal workers in the outdoor hospitality industry are currently giving pay packages (wages plus benefits) ranging from $8 to $12 per hour in order to remain competitive. Jobs that need formal education and/or certification, as well as those with managerial or supervisory duties, should pay at the higher end of this range, if not more.

Keep in mind that Workamping refers to any type of labor that is done while living in an RV. Many Workampers have careers that are unrelated to outdoor hospitality. Some people simply opt to continue working or running a business while living the Workamper lifestyle. You can anticipate to earn as least as much as you are presently earning in these conditions. If on-site camping is not an option, some businesses may typically help you find a parking spot, or you may be on your own to find a parking spot.

Season

The Workamping Season

What is the Workamping Season, exactly? Is it the same as when you go camping? Is it true that all Workamper employers hire for the same amount of time? These are common queries, as there has been some misunderstanding about the definition of the Workamper Season... let's clear things up!

Workamping Season runs concurrently with camping season, which begins around Memorial Day and ends shortly after Labor Day. Employers recruit for a range of start and end dates, and they may even ask you to start in the spring or stay through the winter, so the exact dates aren't necessary.

Jobs abound during the Workamping Season. Employers are frequently overwhelmed by the amount of interest in their available positions and the response to their advertisements. Overall, competition is higher, but it can be especially fierce in locations like Alaska, Seattle, Maine, and National Parks.

Start applying early in the fall/winter and you'll be able to get a leg up on the competition. Make a list of summer jobs before spring arrives to ensure you receive the appropriate job. The Workamping Season is the most convenient time to look for work. The winter, on the other hand, presents a greater problem, therefore we'll spend the majority of this chapter delving into those specifics.

The Winter Season

Family dinners, holiday parties, and the end of the Camperforce season all signal the start of the next leg of the Workamping adventure...the Winter Season...for many Workampers.

It's not uncommon for people to workamp in the winter. It will need a little more organization and forethought than the traditional method of finding a Workamping Season job!

The Workamper chooses to settle into monthly stays at snowbird-friendly parks in the south and far west, still wondering if they could have found a job for the winter instead. The Winter Season brings a bucket load of questions, tons of uncertainty, and even some restlessness as the Workamper chooses to settle into monthly stays at snowbird-friendly parks in the south and far west, still wondering if they could have found a job for the winter instead.

The notion that Workamping is minimal – if not non-existent – during the winter is one not to be taken lightly. If you're ready to venture outside your comfort zones, plan ahead, and maybe use some ingenuity to locate a career you like, it's far from the reality.

Lifestyle

As more people take to the streets and realize that traveling in an RV is what they really want to do, a growing number of people are unfamiliar with the Workamping lifestyle. Workamping has exploded in popularity, and with it has come a slew of new myths, biases, and generalized assumptions. As more millennials and working-age RVers transition into the lifestyle, the notion that you have to be retired and live off your savings income or monthly retirement checks has been discredited. Other fears like realistic living expenditures, working for your site, and being overqualified for basic jobs add to the anxiety of new Workampers before they embark on their major adventures!

Entering the world of Workamping can be a thrilling and enjoyable experience! I remember when we initially started, we were giddy with the prospect of having complete control over our location and fantasizing about discovering hidden nooks and crannies throughout the globe to explore with our children. Workingamping gave us the freedom to come and go as we pleased. It allowed us to explore America on our own terms while also earning some money. If you first comprehend how it all works, it can and will do the same for you!

Making Sense of Dollars

Workamping is a unique way of life. For some, it's a way of life, while for others, it's a mode of transportation. For the majority of people, a combination of the two appears to provide the best of all worlds. When you have little income from outside sources such as tiny enterprises or low-paying hobbies, workamping can be your ticket to travel. It can allow you to hit the road and stay afloat before retiring, as long as you're ready to make required modifications to how much you pay out in relation to the money you receive.

Living in an RV can obviously reduce your living expenses and free up funds for pleasant things like exploring your new area, but it can also provide the essential slack to pay off debt for certain people. This has shown to be true for many people, and they continue to use it as such.

Over the years, one item that has been steady, if not quite constant, has been the cost of RVing. It isn't possible to live for free!

It can be less expensive than a traditional travel lifestyle involving hotels, and it can even compete with the American Dream of having a home in the suburbs, but let's be clear: it's not free living!

Many of the costs of RV travel can be considerably lowered, if not entirely eliminated, by choosing to Workamp along the way. Workamping assists RVers in saving money on expenses like as lodging, site rental, paying for electricity at monthly sites, and needing to pay for onsite facilities. Another significant cost savings is fuel, as you will not be moving your RV from place to place every day when Workamping. In reality, Workamping will allow you to stay in some of the most desirable areas in the United States for extended periods of time, with only local driving required.

Workamping Resume Photos

Many businesses will request that you submit a photograph of yourself and your rig with your résumé. Many Workampers are immediately put off by this approach and wonder if it's simply a form of prejudice for whatever reason. I have to state that I am torn between agreeing and disagreeing with the propriety of providing photos to potential employers. And while I have engaged (in my own way) and urged others to participate in this recruiting activity, it was for one and only one reason: to avoid myself or any other Workamper showing up at a job site only to be turned away.

My husband and I never wanted to come at a new Workamper position with an old motorhome and four kids in tow, not knowing precisely what they were getting. I used to politely decline to submit images, instead including a link to our blog and an offer for the employer to get to know us... I promised myself I would never drive anywhere until I had clearly laid out in an email with a time stamp that we had four kids, this is what we look like, and this is what we camp in. After two instances where the employer was surprised upon arrival that we were so young and had multiple children, even though they still worked out well, I promised myself I would never drive anywhere until I had clearly laid out in an email with a time stamp that we had four kids, this is what we look like, and this is what we camp in

With the lingering anxiety of refusal or rejection, I couldn't imagine driving any distance. This is what I tell people when they ask why I think Workampers should just send the images.

Employers who hire workampers do so virtually. They are not conducting traditional interviews, which would require you to attend at least one face-to-face meeting. Do yourself a favor and submit the images or agree to a virtual interview over Skype or FaceTime in exchange for not having to fly to their office for an in-person interview, which I was once asked to do!

Photos that are considered acceptable for employer review:
- Professional headshot
- Basic headshot
- Selfie showing the full face
- Outdoor pictures with 1/2 body
- Indoor picture with 1/2 body
- Professional full body shot
- Selfie with multiple people showing full face.

Photos that are not considered acceptable for employer review:

- Action shot where you are barely visible
- Outdoor photo of just scenery
- Multiple persona selfie with partial face
- Pictures where your tongue is sticking out
- Full body shots in anything other less than business casual
- Pictures where you are making a funny face, such as a pouty lip

Single RV Workers

I realize it's not always simple to locate RV businesses willing to hire only one individual to work at a campsite! Couples appear to be the luckiest people on the planet!

But believe me when I say that if you want to find work camping employers who are seeking for single working RVers, you've come to the right place!

Workamping Jobs for Singles

I'll start at the beginning by discussing the distinction between single and solo work campers, then give you 30 options for generating money on the road, followed by a list of RV employers you may investigate to help you locate the job you want.

Many Americans of all ages like workamping because it leads to an adventurous life of travel.

Traveling from place to location, state to state, and job to job may not be for everyone, but for many people, it allows them to live the adventurous life they've always wanted while also earning a little income.

Workamping Singles v. Solos

Many RVers today travel as couples, and occasionally as families with children in tow, sharing the obligations of each new employment as well as the lifestyle responsibilities of trip planning, driving, and the less-than-glamorous tasks associated with setting up their campsite. However, not all RVers travel in pairs, and those who do typically have extra concerns about finding businesses willing to hire just one.

While these concerns are legitimate, they are a touch overdone in light of the typically negative social media posts that dominate the scene.

Workamping Jobs for Singles: Knowing the Difference

First, let's define the difference between a solo Work Camper and a single Work Camper.

- The term "single" refers to a scenario in which just one person is capable of or ready to work. This individual may or may not be traveling alone. They are a single Work Camper, which means they work by themselves.

- Someone who is traveling alone is referred to as a solo. They work and travel independently.

In my experience, many firms would do their hardest to fill positions with couples just because they can obtain two workers who can only work on one place. It's not about you; it's about your business. They're attempting to reduce their expenditures by utilizing the expertise and labor power of two people rather than simply one.

What you need to know is that employers are looking for both, those who can fill one spot and those who fill two.

Solo & Single Projects When it comes to people who travel, campers may not be the majority, but the reality is that many wonderful people do so on their own, and their numbers are growing!

Many businesses recruit only one employee per location.

Some businesses only have one open position, or they wish to avoid the chance of personal troubles spilling over into the workplace, therefore they refuse to recruit those who live or travel together.

It benefits you in either case. If you embrace these occupations and possibilities, you'll discover that you have a wide range of options to pick from.

Workamping Jobs for Singles: What's Available?

There are a variety of RV employers and income opportunities available for Solo & Single travelers. A mix of negotiation skills, creativity and patience is almost always a requirement.

30 Workamping Jobs for Singles Ideas

1. Rides Operator
2. Lifeguard
3. Activity Director
4. Food Service Staff
5. Store Clerk
6. Campground Host
7. Raft Guide
8. Tour Guide
9. Docent
10. Groundskeeper
11. Security
12. Gas Line Inspector
13. RV Delivery Driver
14. Mystery Shopper
15. RV Inspector
16. Gate Guard/Attendant
17. Warehouse Worker

18. RV Tech
    19. RV Detailing
    20. Disaster Relief Worker
21. Shuttle Driver
    22. Ski Instructor
    23. Event/Fair Staff
    24. Sporting Event Staff
    25. Pet Grooming
    26. Pet Walker/Sitter
    27. Writer/Blogger
    28. Photographer
    29. Advertising Sales
    30. Campground Map Sale

Who Offers Workamping Jobs for Singles?

Many employers hire only one RVer; some simply do not disclose this explicitly in their job postings. Others clearly prefer to hire two strong workers to fill one RV site, but single workers are welcomed with open arms wherever possible. Many firms would prefer to hire one strong worker rather than a duo where one half is considered as a thorn, therefore do your best to constantly inquire about the availability of hiring one person.

The following employers, among many more, have said that they have opportunities available for Single and Solo Work Campers.

Various Locations:

- S. Army Corps of Engineers
- Texas Advertising – AGS Publishing
- Southeast Publications
- Express Employment Professionals
- Kitchen Craft
- Amazon Camperforce
- Bowlin Travel Centers

- Southern Cross Corp
- KOA: Kampground of America
- Equity Lifestyle Services/Thousand Trails
- Sky Thunder Fireworks

State Specific Locations

- Xanterra Glacier National Park Lodges
- California Land Management
- Yogi Bear Camp Resort Wisconsin Dells
- Adventureland Amusement Park, Iowa
- Delaware North at Yellowstone
- Black Meadow Landing, California
- Greenlaw's RV & Tenting Park, Maine
- Yellowstone Silver Co., Montana
- Yellow Jacket Campground, Florida
- Lakeside Camp Park, Michigan
- Klink's Resort, Washington
- Vermilion Valley Resort, California
- Trinity Pines, Texas
- Indigo Bluffs RV Resort, Michigan
- The Cabins at Historic Columbine, Colorado
- Country Oaks Campground, New Jersey
- Cherry Hill Park, Maryland
- Black Bear Campground, New York
- Chocorua Camping Village, New Hampshire
- Three Rivers Resort, Colorado
- Mackinaw Mill Creek Camping, Michigan
- Pine River Lodge, Colorado
- Cottonwood Borco Ranch, South Dakota
- West Crooked Lake Resort, Minnesota
- Shenandoah Hills Campground, Virginia
- Spring Creek Campground, Montana
- Forest Recreation Mgmt., South Dakota

- Olis Trolley, Maine
- Jack's Campers, South Dakota
- Wall Drug Store, South Dakota
- Canyon Enterprises, Inc., Colorado
- Blue Bonnet RV Resort, Texas
- Okefenokee Swamp Park, Georgia
- Wilderness Aware Rafting, Colorado
- Rocky Mountain HI RV Park, Montana
- Partridge Hollow Campground, Massachusetts
- Treeland Resorts, Wisconsin
- Stonebridge RV Park, Texas
- Reelfoot National Wildlife Refuge, Tennessee
- Jekyll Island Campground, Georgia
- Sportsman's Supply Campground & Mountain Cabins, Colorado
- Sundance 1 Resorts, Arizona
- Corrington Enterprises, Alaska
- North Rim Country Store, Arizona
- YMCA of the Rockies, Colorado
- The Willamettans, Oregon
- Olive Branch Campground, Ohio
- Forever Resorts Parry Lodge, Utah
- Guadalupe-Blanco River Authority, Texas
- Taylor Park Trading Post, Colorado
- Detroit Greenfield RV Park, Michigan
- Idaho State Parks
- Glamis North Hot Springs Resort, California
- River View RV Park, Louisiana
- Cedar Pass Lodge, South Dakota
- Camp McPherson, Ohio

With Kids

If you want to work traditional Workamping jobs like we did, there are a few things you should know before starting your search. After all, Workamping with kids is a little different than going alone or as a couple, and it'll be a lot easier if you know the answers to the most frequently asked questions ahead of time. Workingamping while living in an RV with kids versus doing other digital remote jobs is also a very different experience.

While no two situations are exactly same, here are the top four:

1. Can Both Parents Work?

Both parents can work while traveling, regardless of whether they need child care for younger children. This can be done in a variety of ways, all of which revolve on your personal preferences. My husband and I both work opposite shifts so that we may easily work for the same company. We'd look for job in different areas and ask whether one of us might work in the morning and the other in the evening. We weren't concerned about having the same off days because we knew it would only be temporary, but it turned out to be a nice change for those who preferred the same shifts. It was always a win-win situation for us!

A Few Things to Note:

- A typical workweek consisted of roughly 20-30 hours per person. While working for Amazon Camperforce, we only worked 40 hours (or more).
- We made the most of our working hours by only taking tasks that included a free campground.
- Working opposite shifts becomes tiresome after a while. Because you don't have the same off days as your partner, and you start your shift when they finish theirs, you won't see each other very often.
- It was easier to manage when we limited our visits to four months or less at these job sites.

2. How Much Will I Make?

I try to be up front and honest about this subject, and I'm sure I've mentioned it before, but Workamping will not make you wealthy. You will be paid a respectable pay and, in some cases, given a FREE website if you get a good job, but you will not be contributing to your savings account or retirement fund in any way. If Workamping is your only source of income and you're traveling with children, money will be scarce, and the adventure will be overshadowed by financial difficulties. Find ways to supplement your income with a well-planned small business or revenue-generating pastime, commonly known as a side hustle.

3. Is It Harder Finding Jobs?

I can't say it's more difficult because I've never had a problem. I can't say it was simple because getting the jobs we sought required a lot of well-crafted emails and a fantastic interview. Workamping with children differs from workamping without children. To be successful, you must approach it differently and know how to present yourself.

When you notice a job posting for a campsite position, for example, you need to act a little faster than usual. You don't have time to consider all of the details. Take a short glance at the job posting to see whether it's something you can accomplish, and then apply. You can do more research once you've submitted your application or résumé.

In your email to the company, include how you are enthusiastic about the opportunity to join the team at a family-friendly establishment, some specifics about the adults seeking for work, perhaps a recent accomplishment, and then indicate that you are part of a traveling family with x number of children.

Tell the employer about your background and why you'd be a good fit for the team. I generally included a line about how we didn't require the same days off every week, but that alternate shifts was desirable. Include photos of you and your family, as well as your RV, or include a link to your blog so people may 'meet' your family.

Attach your CV, which should include relevant work experience or just previous roles that highlight your abilities. When it comes to family Workampers, I feel it's better to send too little information and hope they'll ask the correct questions than to send too much information and hope they'll ask the right questions.

4. Can Kids Come To Work?

This is such a complicated topic, and I don't believe it can be solved solely through common sense and good judgment. Bringing small children or even younger teenagers into the workplace involves a variety of criteria, but at least three of them must work flawlessly together, which is rare.

- You're assuming they'll behave, be helpful, and be happy for the duration of your shift without your continual supervision or hovering over them.
- If your employer agrees, they are presuming that your children are well behaved (according to the company's expectations), that they will not interfere with your work, and that they may even be able to assist you.
- Everyone assumes that the children are aware of how to act in a professional atmosphere, that they are aware of their function, and that they are aware of the expectations established by you and your company.

So, I suppose it all depends on what you're doing, where you work, and what the property's rules are. Keep in mind that it could be feasible one day and completely unreasonable the next.

I recommend approaching the situation with an open mind. If bringing the kids to work with you is the only way to make it work, be open and honest with your boss from the start. You never want to travel any distance if the chance of being turned away or being asked to leave sooner than intended exists.

Homeschooling for kids

There are several large lifestyle changes to be made if you choose to take up full-time RVing, especially if you are bringing the children along on your cross-country adventures. Not only do you have to worry about housing and feeding everyone in a limited space, but you also have your children's' education. Basic education is required by law for children up to a certain age, anywhere from 16 to 18 depending on your home state's laws.

Full-timers with children will have to set up some homeschooling system, RV travel homeschool if you will. Let's look at homeschooling while on the road such as some of the benefits, drawbacks, and resources for the family.

Starting Your Own RV Homeschooling Program

The good news for parents and children is that homeschooling in an RV doesn't have to be dramatically different than any other type of schooling. You have less space to work with, in a brick and mortar home you may have an entire room set apart as the classroom but that will not be feasible in even a large motorhome. RVing offers a unique opportunity for an on the road education your children will never find in a traditional classroom setting, no matter where in the US you call home.

One of your first challenges will be devoting a space or being able to transform an area into a temporary classroom setting, having a particular layout or design devoted to learning will increase the overall effectiveness of an on the road education.

When it comes to an RV, you may not necessarily have the dedicated space you'd like to do this. This is where thinking outside the box and using laptops and tablets may be helpful.

What Are the Benefits of RV Homeschooling?

Homeschooling on the road does provide its own unique set of benefits. Life on the road creates a dynamic and creative learning environment where you can cater to a child's learning experience. For example, you may decide to do a lesson on geological activity while at Yellowstone National Park or go through the history of the Civil War while at the Gettysburg battle site.

This dynamic and hands-on learning has been shown to be beneficial to a child's growing mind. The shifting landscape and non-linear learning could keep your child more focused on the task at hand.

The other advantages of RV homeschooling are some of the same benefits that come with traditional homeschool. Benefits such as educational, physical and emotional freedoms, the ability to operate on your schedule and the ability to make changes should something need to be changed.

Many parents and children who homeschool also report closer ties and stronger relationships compared to those students and parents in traditional school settings. Students who have also homeschooled regularly outperform traditional students when it comes to standardized testing such as the ACT or SAT.

What Are the Drawbacks of RV Homeschooling?

One of the most significant drawbacks of RV homeschooling, other than the smaller size, of course, may have to do with one of the big advantages. Life on the road is one of constant change, while this change seems to be beneficial it is always nice to add a bit of stability now and then.

The other drawbacks to RV homeschooling are the same drawbacks of homeschooling in general. Coming up with lesson plans, being both parents and teacher and trying to become experts on all subjects can become quite stressful on the parent. Ensuring your children balance school work with physical activity can be challenging, too, depending on how long you're on the road and where you're traveling to. Make sure to plan outdoor time when the weather's appropriate based on where your RV adventures take you.

An essential part of school for children is learning to interact with other children, something they won't get with homeschooling, especially on the road. When choosing destinations and places to stay, it's important to find ones that allow your children to interact with other children on the road.

Deciding to hit the road full-time and the decision to homeschool your children are both major lifestyle changes that require plenty of research and careful thought before executing. Make sure you talk to plenty of other road schooling RVers to get an idea of what life on the road and teaching your children on the road is like.

With pets

For many people, life is simply more enjoyable when they have furry buddies to share it with. When you live in an RV full-time, this is even more true, because traveling with a pet means you have an excited little someone—or a huge one, depending on the situation—to share all of your fantastic adventures with. Living in an RV allows you to spend a lot of time with your family and pets, which leads to a lot of hilarious and important images being taken virtually every day, if not every hour. When you look back decades from now, preserving these memories in a photo album for your pets or family or a photobook will make you cherish the times.

If you're planning to hit the road soon and want to bring your family pet with you, or if you're currently on the road and want to get a dog, cat, or other pet for your family to enjoy, you might be wondering what to expect when living in a full-time RV with pets. Get them a giftbox from petboxsubs to keep them from moving around too much while traveling. Natural food, a healthy toy, and a pet accessory are all included in the box. The truth is that no two animals are alike, thus your experience may differ from that of the next person. However, there are several important considerations to make before bringing any animal into your RV.

In this section, we'll go through those topics and offer our best advice on living in an RV with a pet. These pointers will assist you in making the most of your transition and future travels.

Choosing the Right Pet

Let's begin by discussing how to choose an ideal travel companion. Picking the right pet can make all the difference in how successful you are with this venture.

First, you will need to decide on the type of animal you would like to keep. Dogs and cats tend to be the most popular options and are probably the easiest animals to travel with. That said, some families choose to travel with fish and/or birds. Doing so just takes a bit more creativity and planning when it comes to moving day.

If you do decide to go the dog route, make sure you know which breeds might be turned down at campgrounds. Generally speaking, these include breeds that are considered "aggressive" such as pit bulls. While the pit bull you choose may not be aggressive in the least, many campgrounds are not willing to budge when it comes to rules, which can lead to frustrating situations for your family.

Once you know what kind of animal you want, you can begin shopping around. While doing this, you'll want to keep in mind the personality of any pet you choose:

- Do you want your puppy to be able to run about freely?
- Will you be able to meet their needs?
- Have you fallen in love with an outdoor-loving cat?

- When they're in campgrounds, how will you allow kids to spend time outside?

Answering these kinds of questions before making any final judgments will assist you avoid picking an animal that won't fit into your travel lifestyle.

This section obviously does not apply to you if your family already has a pet that they plan to bring along. In this scenario, we just suggest that you think about your pet's personality and demands. If you have a dog who barks a lot, a cat who gets motion sickness, or a reptile who needs continual heat from a lamp, you might consider finding a new home for your pet. Otherwise, you'll have to be ready to face some more hurdles.

Keeping Your Pet Comfortable

Your pet's comfort and safety are of the utmost concern. As a result, you'll want to do everything you can to make sure your pet is comfortable in your RV. Providing a bed, playthings, food and water, and a place to relieve themselves in an RV isn't much different than it would be in a stick-and-bricks home for the most part.

Here are a few things to think about if you're driving an RV:

- **Get a ramp:** smaller dogs may struggle to enter and exit your RV. A small ramp is an ideal solution if this is the case.
- **Go on walks:** Because your pet won't be able to run around freely in the campground, daily walks are essential for their comfort and wellbeing.
- **Provide your pet a space:** RVs can be rather claustrophobic. This means your pet will likely be underfoot a lot, which can make them feel uneasy. Find a corner for your pet to call their own to solve this problem.

Traveling With Your Furry Friend

The next thing to address is the process of traveling from one place to the next with your pet. This might prove to be slightly challenging at first. However, as your family finds their groove and your pet learns the routine, travel days will become easier and easier.

Here are some things to keep in mind when preparing to move your rig with pets:

- **Move animals out of your trailer:** While traveling, no living thing should be left in a bumper pull or fifth wheel. It's risky to leave a pet in your trailer because items tend to shift during transport. Furthermore, without heat or air conditioning, the trailer's temperature could pose a problem.

- **Be prepared for motion sickness:** Motion sickness affects some dogs and cats. Keeping a few of these medications on hand could save your family's life.
- **Ease jumpy animals into moving day:** Your pet may become agitated by the sounds of a motorhome's engine or simply being in the truck. If you think this would be an issue, start the engine or have your animal sit in the truck a few times before the trip.
- **Stop often and look for pet-friendly stops:** Traveling with dogs, in particular, will necessitate numerous stops. Look for places that allow dogs to run and play, clean up any messes your pet makes, and make sure to bring food and water with you at all times.

Leaving Your Animal at Home Alone

Getting out and seeing the sights is a big part of the fun of traveling. Unfortunately, pets aren't always — or even typically — permitted to accompany you to the attractions. As a result, you'll have to leave them alone at home.

This can cause anxiety in pet owners for a multitude of reasons. They may be concerned that the electricity may be turned off, leaving their pet exposed to extremely high temperatures. They may also be concerned that their cat will become scared and destroy their belongings, or that their dog will bark nonstop, annoying their neighbors.

To relax your thoughts, try some of these techniques:

- **Use a crate:** If you're concerned that your pet will become agitated while you're away, consider using a crate. Just make sure the crate is big enough for your pet and don't leave them alone for too long.
- **Chat with the neighbors:** Go ahead and strike up a conversation with your next-door neighbors. Tell them you'll be gone and that you don't know how your pet will respond. Request that they notify you if they see excessive barking so that you can take actions to prevent it in the future.
- **Invest in a temperature alert system:** The use of a temperature monitor like this one will provide you peace of mind. If the temperature drops too low or rises too high, this system will send an alert to your phone.
- **Provide necessities:** Even if you don't expect to be gone for long, make sure your pet has food, drink, and a place to empty themselves if necessary. This can help you avoid complications if something prevents you from coming home as soon as you planned.

- **Lock doors and windows:** If you don't want to crate your pet, make sure all doors and windows are locked before leaving the house. You don't want your darling kitty or treasured dog to escape.

Finding Pet-Friendly Campgrounds

While there are many pet-friendly campgrounds, some do not allow particular dog breeds, and others do not allow pets at all. As a result, you should always do your homework before visiting a new RV park.

Use the website BringFido to identify pet-friendly campgrounds. It's also a good idea to stay within a specific campsite system that welcomes pets. For example, all Thousand Trails parks welcome dogs and cats to join their visitors. Are you undecided about where you want to stay? Make a reservation in advance.

Keep in mind that many pet-friendly campgrounds will request confirmation of immunizations before allowing your pet into the park. As a result, you should always have your pet's vaccination record on hand while checking in.

Respecting Your Neighbors

While vacationing in an RV park, it is always crucial to respect your neighbors. Remember that not everyone is an animal lover, and that not everyone will appreciate your dog running around on their property.

Following these easy pet etiquette standards will allow you, your pet, and your neighbors to live in peace:

1. At all times, keep your pet on a leash.
2. Stop your dog from barking all the time, especially after hours.
3. Clean up after your pet at all times.

Chapter 6: Boondocking

What is Boondocking?

Boondocking is a simpler form of camping in certain ways. You save the reservation process and fees, but you forego the convenience of a developed campground.

Boondocking is also a convenient way to simply park your vehicle and sleep. Parking at a free lot overnight can save you time and money if you're on a tight schedule and only need a place to crash for the night.

There are a range of free and low-cost camping choices depending on why and how you want to boondock.

Boondocking is a general camping phrase, but it is more frequent among the RV, van life, and Overlanding communities because they have the necessary supplies and storage. Whether vehicle camping or boondocking in a Class A RV, anyone can boondock. If you plan on boondocking frequently, consider purchasing charged external batteries, a composting toilet, a freshwater tank, and solar panels.

Why boondock?

By definition, boondocking is staying overnight with no or limited hookups. The other phrase is "dry camping," which refers to remaining without electricity for two or more days. Both words are used interchangeably by RVers. For a variety of circumstances, you may find yourself boondocking or dry camping. When you're done with this one, go over to my other essay, "Boondocking Required," to discover why and when you'll be in this predicament.

The Epitome of Convenience

Because it is more convenient, we frequently choose to boondock. When we first started keeping track, we were boondocking an average of 11 nights per month in 2006, 12 nights per month in 2007, 11 nights per month in 2008, and 12 nights per month in 2009. We still boondocking approximately 10 nights per month, on average, 7 years later—whenever and whenever it is easy to do, i.e. convenient.

You may certainly save money by boondocking because campsite fees are waived. Campgrounds, on the other hand, provide services that you may require on occasion. I'm not a fan of boondocking for the majority of the time (or all of the time, as some people do) solely to save money. This will necessitate a shift in your lifestyle, which I believe will be detrimental. We don't want to do it, and we don't support it.

Where and Why to Boondock

At rallies and RV gatherings, you may be obliged to boondock (camp for several days). There are frequently no hookups or, at best, merely power at the site.

Quartzsite, Arizona hosts the world's largest RV gathering every January, and boondocking is a must for the 10-day stay. Even getting your RV serviced may necessitate a one- or two-night stay, with no or limited connections. We're hooked into an outlet just outside a service bay, and if the servicing isn't finished by the time the techs leave for the day, we might have to spend the night here.

We were traveling with companions and used a field to park in for a few days, despite the fact that it was not a required like service or Quartzsite (with permission, of course). A relative of mine owns the property. From our coaches, we could see deer and wild turkey. What a beautiful and practical website.

My RV, like yours, has those self-contained features, which we take advantage of. When you have the capacity to boondock, you have access to hundreds of places to stay that you would otherwise have to avoid if you had convinced yourself that you needed to hook up to utilities for the night.

If I really need to stop (tired, sleepy, hungry, etc.), I don't want to have to travel another 20-30 miles simply to find a campground or feel obligated to hook up to utilities. That's simply not safe. I also don't want to be forced to drive a predetermined distance simply because I made a reservation.

I'm not anti-campsite; when I require the services that the campground provides (utilities and space), I pay the money, stay there, and appreciate the chance. Consider this: I only go to the grocery store when I need groceries, the barbershop when I need a haircut, and campgrounds when I require camping services. When we spend two or more nights in one location, I also use campgrounds.

The Ultimate in Instant Savings

Because you keep the money in your pocket, boondocking will result in immediate and big cost reductions. If you assume a nightly campground cost of $30.00 and boondocking one night per week, you will save more than $1,500 a year ($30.00 X 52 weeks = $1,560). In 2009, we slept an average of 2.75 nights each week on a 12-nights-per-month basis. By multiplying (2.75 x $1,560 = $4,290), the savings from boondocking for that many nights was significant. This kind of savings will more than cover the expense of extra fuel and allow you to keep RVing.

Let's get this party started! Even you must admit that a sum of almost $4,000 is not to be taken lightly!

Public Boondocking sites

There are numerous places where you are legally permitted to stay overnight. If you're out in the woods, the best way to find a safe boondock place is to go somewhere remote, like BLM land. Here are some additional popular possibilities if you're in town and need to find free camping quickly:

- **Walmart Parking Lots**

Boondocking is allowed in any Walmart parking lot for up to 24 hours at a time. You can stock up on supplies while parking for free by boondocking here.

You're quite conspicuous, and security is usually present in most parking lots. However, Walmart's restrictions on boondocking are tightening, so check with the exact location before thinking it's OK. There's even an app that will help you discover a Walmart that allows boondocking!

- **Truck Stops/Rest Areas**

RVers and Van campers are welcome to remain overnight at several truck stops and rest areas. However, because there is normally little monitoring here, make sure someone knows where you are. You'll be near to a restroom and off the beaten path. Although traffic can be noisy, certain rest sites in more remote places can feel a lot like campers!

- **Visitors Centers**

During the night, visitor centers are frequently uninhabited and may even offer running water and restrooms. Before committing to boondocking at a visitor center, make sure to check with them first.

- **Trail Heads**

Overnight backpacking expeditions are popular on many paths. As a result, it's not uncommon to find vehicles parked overnight at trailheads.

- **Hotels/Motels**

It's always a risk boondocking in a hotel or motel parking lot. Many prominent hotels will be unconcerned if their parking lot are already nearly vacant. If the lot is full, it's advisable to keep looking because you don't want to be towed.

- **National Forests**

Boondocking doesn't have to include parking in a sketchy area. It's a terrific method to boondock in the woods by parking off of forest service roads. There's more on this below!

Select Your Rig

So you've made the decision to live in your RV full-time. Congratulations! All you have to do now is choose the best rig for your needs. Doesn't it appear to be simple? Not so fast, my friend. There are a plethora of RV models to pick from, and the changes between them may appear minor, but they can make a significant difference in how happy you are on the road.

Full-time RVing necessitates careful consideration of how you use your space, especially if you work from home, have major interests, or are traveling with a family.

When looking for an RV for full-time RVing, the first thing to think about is how you intend to spend your time. What type of full-time RVing lifestyle do you desire? Do you want to park in one spot and never leave, or do you want to see every state in the United States in a year? Answering those questions will assist you in determining the size (or size) of RV you desire and require. If you're only going to be in one area, size doesn't really matter. If you want to be mobile, though, smaller and lighter is preferable. You must also consider the vehicle you will use while full-time RVing. Will you be towing a trailer or driving an RV? In either case, you'll need a big vehicle to haul your trailer or a compact car to tow your RV behind it.

Next, consider how you'll make use of your area. Do you require dedicated office space for working from home, including a computer, printer, and other office supplies? Do you require a storage facility for bicycles, power equipment, or skis? Do you plan on bringing a motorcycle or other "toys" with you? When full-time RVing, it's critical to consider how much space each person in the RV actually requires.

Examine your RV storage area to see how you can make the most of it. A few shelves here and there, or some wall hooks there, can make a big difference. Measure the closets and cabinets, if possible, and compare them to what you have at home. Also, check to see whether things like your kitchen dishes or your favorite sauté pan will fit.

Consider the environment. Do you want to spend your time in a place where it is hot for the most of the year, or do you want to experience all four seasons? Examine the RV's insulation, the size of the air conditioner and heaters, the amount of power required to run those systems, and whether you'd be comfortable year-round wherever you are.

Do you prefer "glamping" or "camping"? To put it another way, do you want to spend the majority of your time on paved campgrounds with full hookups and facilities such as a pool and clubhouse? Or are you planning on boondocking (camping without electricity) in more rural areas? If you choose the latter, make sure you have a generator or solar power source and that you understand how all of your systems operate. Last but not least, don't be hesitant to ask questions. Take a trip through an RV park in your neighborhood, or at your next vacation destination, and ask some of the campers what they enjoy and don't like about their RVs. Visit several sellers and conduct thorough research. The most crucial step in beginning your new lifestyle is selecting the perfect "home on wheels" for full-time RVing.

Monitoring and charging your betteries

Things You Need To Know About Your RV Battery

Your RV battery system is an important part of the interior setup of your vehicle. Everything electronic in your coach, from your overhead vent fan to your HVAC system to your refrigerator, is powered by it.

It's critical to recognize that your RV coach battery is made up of two separate systems: a 120-volt AC system and a 12-volt DC system. If you're driving a motorhome, you'll have a conventional car battery to start the engine, just like you would in a typical passenger vehicle.

The 120 volt system is the more powerful battery, which is used to drive major equipment in electric mode, such as your rooftop air conditioner or refrigerator. To use this battery, you must be either connected to shore power (like you would be in a developed campground) or running an electrical generator capable of charging such a large battery. (Generating that much power with solar is difficult, which is why running your air conditioner on solar is nearly impossible!)

When you're plugged up, running your generator, or actually driving, the 12-volt coach system charges. This smaller battery system powers items like overhead fans, inside lights, and the water system, and it can be utilized without a generator even when the RV isn't linked up – until the battery dies, that is.

Let's go into the nitty gritty on some of the most common inquiries about the RV battery system now that we have a basic idea of what it looks like.

1. What is the best RV battery?

There are a variety of RV battery options on the market, and depending on which campers you ask, you'll likely hear passionate arguments for and against each type. Here are a few of the most popular options:

- **Deep-cycle batteries** are lead-acid batteries that are comparable to those found in boats and golf carts. It's similar to a car battery in that it creates and retains power using the same chemistry, but a deep-cycle battery produces a constant amount of current over a longer period of time, whereas car batteries produce a lot of current in a short period of time (since they charge while you're driving anyway). Floating wet-cell batteries, absorbed glass mat (AGM) batteries, and gel-type batteries are all examples of deep cycle batteries. Each has its own peculiarities and maintenance requirements.

- **Lithium batteries** are an alternative to traditional lead-acid batteries, including the deep-cycle batteries offered with most modern RVs. Many campers who rig their RVs for solar power generation upgrade to lithium batteries, which, though expensive, offer a variety of benefits over other types: they're lighter in weight, smaller, and don't require the same kind of tedious maintenance other types of batteries do. (For example, wet cell batteries require you to check and replenish electrolyte levels, whereas lithium batteries are set-it-and-forget-it.) Lithium batteries also have a much longer lifespan than other battery types, and are typically rated for 5,000 cycles — as opposed to the 400 or so cycles most lead-acid batteries get. That said, they cost approximately three times more up front, which keep them out of the reach of some campers.

2. What is an RV Battery Bank?

No, batteries do not have their own banking institution; a battery bank is what you get when you combine two or more batteries. When you need additional power, you can increase the voltage or amps.

RV batteries in series

By connecting RV batteries in series, you may maintain the same amperage while increasing the voltage. When two 6-volt RV batteries are connected in series, the overall voltage is 12 volts, but the amps stay the same.

To connect RV batteries, a jumper wire is utilized. One battery's negative terminal is linked to the positive terminal of the other. The remaining positive and negative terminals are connected to whatever you're attaching the batteries to with another set of connections. The voltage and amp rating of connected batteries should be the same.

RV batteries in parallel

A parallel RV battery bank boosts current while maintaining the same voltage. You can get 6 volts by connecting two 6-volt RV batteries in parallel, but the amps will be increased. Two positive terminals are connected to two negative terminals to form a parallel connection. As a result, a negative negative and a positive positive are created. The batteries can then be attached to your application, and when used, they will drain evenly.

It's also feasible to set up a parallel bank in a series. You can now raise the voltage and amps. A minimum of four batteries are required. Keeping note of the connections you build is a good idea. You can connect as many batteries as you desire, though an RV battery box may be required to keep your individual cells safe and secure. A series power bank can be created by connecting two sets of batteries in parallel.

3. RV Battery Maintenance

The sort of batteries in your RV will have an impact on how well they are maintained. As previously stated, lithium batteries, for example, require almost no maintenance.

Other types of batteries, on the other hand, have varying maintenance requirements and lifespans. If you're traveling with lithium ion batteries versus a wet-cell deep cycle battery, for example, the answer to the question "How long do RV batteries last?" will be considerably different.

Check with the manufacturer of your specific batteries for the most detailed RV battery maintenance guidelines. So, here are some fundamentals.

- **Maintain electrolyte levels in flooded-cell batteries.** With each charge cycle, flooded-cell batteries lose water, and this water must be replaced. To assist prevent sulfation, or the production of sulfate crystals, which can occur when the battery plates are exposed to air, you must use pure water. Before completing the necessary maintenance, check the batteries at least once a month to ensure that they are properly charged.

- **Clean battery terminals:** To get rid of any corrosion that has accumulated. Scrub with a toothbrush using a mixture of one cup of baking soda to a gallon of water or a commercial battery contact cleaning product.
- **Allowing your batteries to get too low in charge can also increase sulfation:** Sulfation might start when your batteries drop below 80%, or 12.4 volts. As a result, make sure to recharge your batteries as soon as possible after each use.
- **Try to recharge your batteries often:** If you discharge your battery to 50% every day, for example, it will last twice as long as if you discharge it to 20% every day. Keep in mind, however, that overcharging and exposure to high temperatures can have a harmful impact on batteries over time.

4. RV Battery Storage

During the winter, most recreational vehicles are kept for several months. If you don't take care of your battery, it will eventually die. Your battery's life will be impacted as a result. Flooded cell batteries die when they are exposed to the cold. It is impossible for a charged battery to become frozen. Although AGM batteries are more resistant to freezing than flooded cell batteries, it is still necessary to avoid this.

Consider disconnecting your vehicle's batteries and bringing them home. Every month, check the voltage and charge if it drops below 80%. It should be sufficient to charge for the night. If you can't remove the batteries from your equipment, there are a few things you can do to keep them alive.

To begin, turn off the power in your home. Radios, refrigerators, smoke alarms, and propane detectors all use tiny milliamps that drain your battery over time. Even if everything is turned off, watts is still being consumed.

As the batteries naturally discharge, charge them. If you have access to your rig while it is being stored, make sure to fully charge the battery every a month. Solar panels that aren't properly regulated may lose their charge or, worse, boil away their electrolyte.

In order to charge the RV batteries, converters should never be left plugged in. This is a surefire technique to quickly evaporate your RV batteries.During storage, keep an eye on your batteries. If you don't change your batteries once a month, you'll have to buy new ones the next season.

5. RV Battery Monitors

Without a monitor, it is difficult to determine the true state of charge of an RV battery. An RV battery monitor can tell you exactly where you are by measuring the amount of energy moving into and out of your battery, as well as its charge or discharge state.

There are many various types of RV battery monitors on the market, and the majority of them may be put into your RV battery system aftermarket. Most modern RV battery monitors come with an LCD display that displays all of the important information regarding your RV battery, as well as additional sophisticated features.

The Victron Battery Monitor, for example, has a temperature sensor and is Bluetooth compatible, so you can use your smartphone to monitor the health of your RV batteries. However, to be accurate, a battery monitor does not need to be flashy or expensive. The AiLi battery monitor, which costs less than $45, is another option. It won't send you updates, but it does make checking the state of your battery as simple as glancing at it!

6. RV Battery Charging

The batteries charge when your RV is plugged into an electrical socket. Every RV is equipped with an RV Converter/Charger, which transforms grid electricity into 12-volt DC and then routes it to the adaptor. Batteries are also charged when your motorhome's (or tow vehicle's) motor is running or when you use your generator. If your RV is connected in, as well as monitoring your RV battery monitor, you'll know your batteries are charging.

While you may absolutely keep your RV plugged in all the time, this will quickly deplete the water levels in your wet-cell batteries, so be sure to check them frequently if you camp this way. Remember that allowing your batteries to become too low in charge might shorten their lifespan, so keep them charged on a regular basis.

7. How much does an RV battery cost?

As previously said, the cost of your batteries varies greatly depending on the type of battery you choose. A single 12-volt wet-cell lead acid battery, for example, might cost several hundred dollars, whereas lithium battery systems can cost thousands. However, because of their longer lifespans, lithium batteries can be more cost-effective in the long run, so if you can afford it up front, it's worth it.

8. How do you install an RV battery?

To install an RV battery, switch off all of the devices that use the battery's power, including small appliances such as overhead lights. Make a mental note of where the present battery is, and then detach the wires, negative first, positive second. If required, clean the wires and the new battery's terminals, then replace the battery and reconnect the cables. Install any hold-down hardware that came with the battery, then test it out!

Helpful things to take

Camping in an RV can be done in a variety of ways. You can stay in a posh resort with an onsite golf course, a state park with woodland sites and easy access to hiking trails, a KOA with loads of kid-friendly activities, or you can leave it all behind and go boondocking for the ultimate RV experience.
Boondocking is a phrase that refers to RVing outside of a campsite with no hookups. It's done a lot in national forests, on BLM land, and even in parking lots.

How to Find Boondocking

- **Campendium:** This is my go-to site for discovering free camping and boondocking opportunities. They feature a large database of various campgrounds, as well as reviews, pricing information, and images. They make it simple to find free campgrounds, and you can search for "free camping" on their website. The finest part about Campendium, though, is the extensive reviews. They record cell signal strength, publish camper images, keep track of current prices, and offer navigational advice for off-the-beaten-path locations. This is always our first destination when seeking for camping on BLM or National Forest land.

- **AllStays:** This application is the best of the best. It costs $10, but one night of free camping pays for it. It maintains one of the most up-to-date boondocking directories on the internet. We usually utilize it to identify parking spots that allow overnight camping at Walmart, Kmart, Lowes, and other stores. The app's evaluations are really helpful in locating the ideal overnight stop.
- **US Public Lands App:** This software, created by RV bloggers Technomadia, lets you locate BLM (Bureau of Land Management) and USFS (US Forest Service) land where you may camp for free. The software charges $2.99 (at the time of writing) and can provide you with a wealth of information about public areas, including how to tell if you've trespassed.
- **Boondockers Welcome:** Boondockers Welcome is the place to go if you want to mooch with strangers. This annual membership is an excellent method to find campgrounds in the driveway. Many of the folks that post properties on Boondockers are RVers and all-around great people.
- **Call the experts:** Get in touch with the pros. Find a BLM regional office in your area and give them a call. Park rangers will be able to provide you with a wealth of information regarding where you can and cannot camp.
- **Check Instagram:** The true professionals. Right now, there's no better place to uncover beautiful boondocking spots than Instagram. My Instagram feed is often flooded with photos of RVs parked on gravel roads in the highlands. If you're looking for amazing boondocking spots, ask those that do it every day! Many travelers are amazing at responding to Instagram comments or will geotag their camping spot so you can add it to your list of future excursions.
- **Boondocking Etiquette:** Before you break out your slides and create a campfire, there are a few laws to follow, whether you're in a parking lot or in the woods.
- **Make sure you're in the right place:** Sites like Campendium will provide precise coordinates so you can park in the correct location. The purpose of boondocking is to enjoy nature rather than ruin it. Make sure to stick to established roads and only camp in designated places.
- **Drive your tow car into new camping spots to scout first:** You can always unhook your tow car and scout a place beforehand if you're apprehensive about

your rig being able to get down a gravel road. This is an excellent strategy to avoid getting caught in a bind. Using Campendium reviews or asking fellow travelers can also be helpful in this situation!

- **Leave no trace:** You won't have a ranger or camp host to make sure you're cleaning up after yourself when you go primitive or wild camping. Don't take advantage of nature. When you're ready to leave, gather your belongings. This also means that when boondocking, you should never dump your black tanks. Never, never, never, never, never, never, never, never, never, never It's not only filthy and harmful for the environment, but it also destroys everyone else's camping experience. Don't be a sour grape!

- **Don't overstay your welcome and be respectful of the surroundings:** There will be restrictions wherever you park. The maximum on most public lands is 14 nights in a 28-day period. On any of the previously mentioned apps and websites, there will be indicators or information about stay limitations. Being courteous and not overstaying your welcome also applies to overnight parking at places like Walmart or Cabela's. The majority of these establishments will let you park for free for one night. Don't have a party outside by opening all of your slides, lowering your jacks, and sliding out your awning. It's also time to lower your jacks, extend your awning, and have a party outside. Before you settle in for the night, go shopping at the store and ask the manager whether you can camp.

- **Check local laws and rules:** Before boondocking, check for fire prohibitions, animal advisories, vehicle limits, and other restrictions.

- **Be respectful of your neighbors:** We made sure to park at the far left end of an open, flat field when boondocking in the Tetons. This not only gave other RVs plenty of room to park, but it also insured that we wouldn't be parked right next to each other. Give your neighbors plenty of room, especially if you're in an open area. While it may seem obvious, you should not listen to loud music or use your generator at all hours of the night. Some campgrounds will have laws prohibiting the use of generators or loud music. However, in general, it is advisable to keep an area's quiet by avoiding these two loud activities.

- **Be conservative:** Supplies are scarce when camping off the grid. Water should be conserved. Don't use a lot of electricity (unless you have solar and know you can handle it). Also, don't overfill your grey and black tanks. For this reason, we have never showered while boondocking. We'll use baby wipes or Epic Wipes, which are

16 times larger than a baby wipe and are ideal for a full-body "shower" when water is limited.
- **Be prepared:** Always empty your grey and black tanks and fill your freshwater tank before boondocking. Purchase groceries and any other items you may require for off-grid camping. Oh, and don't forget to do your laundry! Nothing is worse than running out of underwear and not being able to shower while camping in the mountains.

Chapter BONUS: Additional Resources

RV Clubs and Memberships

I had no idea RV memberships existed until we started RVing. Before retirement, I had no idea full-time RVing was a thing. With little knowledge or experience in the RV world, we decided to go full-time.

Our intention was not to become RVers. Our goal was to travel to each of the fifty states. Purchasing an RV turned out to be the most cost-effective option. So, four days after our wedding, we bought a fixer-upper on Craigslist, plotted our route, and set out.

We wouldn't arrive at a campground until after camp offices closed at 5 p.m. because it took us so long to pack up the RV and hit the road on our first day as RVers. We were immediately confronted with an unexpected problem: how do you check into a campground if no one is there?

The Best RV Club Memberships (in order of how frequently we use ours)

- Passport America
- Harvest Hosts
- Good Sam
- Escapees
- Thousand Trails

Passport America

Passport America is the 50% Discount Camping Club.

Cost

- $44 annually
- $79 for two years
- $109 for three years

Benefits

- 50% off camping fees at participating campgrounds
- Nearly 2,000 participating campgrounds
- Easy-to-use mobile app
- Affiliate referral program

The Problem with Passport America

The parks run by Passport America have a bad reputation for being unfriendly. We've certainly stayed in some filthy $12 parking lots posing as RV parks. We've also stayed at a few RV resorts with pools, hot tubs, high-speed internet, game rooms, and all the other amenities that come with resort RV parks. Passport America has the advantage of allowing you to quickly view amenities. However, you won't be able to see reviews on their app (you'll have to look for them on RV Park Reviews or Google).

Is Passport America worth it?

Passport America pays for itself in two nights or even one use if used in California, where it pays for itself very immediately. Without a doubt, every RVer should join Passport America. Because of PA, we've saved hundreds of dollars, yet membership is so inexpensive! We are lifelong members who have been using the program for the past six years. However, you should not join Passport America solely to save money. PA is also a terrific option to supplement your income while on the road. All referrals to Passport America earn $10 in affiliate commissions. So, if you sign up for Passport America through my link, I'll get $10 for referring you.

This is a fantastic way to advertise a product you use frequently while still earning a little more income. Plus, if you join up a campground for Passport, you can earn some money. In addition, if you refer a campground to Passport America, you can earn up to $100. Anyone who uses PA can create their own affiliate link, allowing you to earn money in this way as well!

Harvest Hosts

Harvest Hosts is a one-night free RV membership that allows campers to park their RV at various wineries, vineyards, breweries, farms, and museums.

Cost

- $79 annually (price changed Jan 2019)

Benefits

- "One" free night of camping

- A good way to meet locals
- 1000+ locations

The Problem with Harvest Hosts

You won't have any form of hookups if you park at HH spots. Plus, as part of the Harvest Hosts arrangement, participating business owners will let you stay for one night. However, I can tell you from personal experience that the nicer you are (and the more wine, beer, and other alcoholic beverages you purchase), the more likely you will be allowed to remain longer, especially during the week or off-season.

Harvest Hosts' previous owners were extremely rigorous about the one-night rule, but the present owners are considerably more relaxed. So you can stay as long as your host will let you at your fantastic Harvest Hosts site. We've only stayed in one place for three nights.

Is Harvest Hosts worth it?

Harvest Hosts theoretically pays for itself in one night. However, the idea behind HH is that in exchange for patronizing the business, you can camp for free (saving yourself at least $35). Because the majority of participating HH companies are wineries, breweries, or farms, this is a terrific way to get to know the area and sample local delicacies.

However, just a few bottles of wine will quickly exceed the cost of a campsite. This isn't the best membership for simply saving money. This isn't the ideal subscription if you're only looking to save money. Your hotel costs will decrease, but your spending will almost certainly increase.

HH is fantastic for meeting new people, visiting a new place, and having a fun night with food and drink!!! (They are so fantastic that they deserve all of the exclamation points!) You can stay at numerous HH sites on the east coast for up to three nights and spend more than $100 on wine tasting, a couple bottles of local wine, and supper. This is more than you had planned to spend on hotels, but you will meet some wonderful people and have a terrific time.

Good Sam Club

Good Sam Club is the company's reward program (it's separate from their insurance and roadside help, and it's not the same as a Sam's Club membership).

Cost

$29 annually

$50 for two years

$79 for three years

Benefits

- 10% off camping fees at participating campgrounds
- Over 2,400 participating campgrounds
- Up to 10% savings at Camping World
- Up to 8¢ off the gallon at select Pilot Flying J locations

The Problem with Good Sam

The camping discount offered by Good Sam is quite minimal. It just costs a few dollars per night, so you'll need to use this membership regularly to recoup your investment. But the correspondence that Good Sam sends is my main gripe with them. There was a TON of mail. All of them are attempting to upsell you on other services, including ones you already use. They send me letters twice a week, attempting to sell me things that I already possess and get me to purchase more. STOP KILLING TREES, I've already given you my money.

Is Good Sam Club worth it?

Good Sam has changed its perks in recent years. It used to offer a three-cent discount per gallon, but that has now been increased to five cents for gas and eight cents for diesel. They used to provide 30% off Camping World purchases, however that number has since been reduced to 10%. By staying at a couple campgrounds and filling up your gas tank at their "select" Pilot Flying J locations, this membership can pay for itself if you use the camping and gas discounts. Pilot Flying J sites that they "choose." We've been using Good Sam for years, and I'm not sure we've ever saved more than $50, however it always pays for itself. I think it's worthwhile, although you can save more money with Passport America (or potentially Harvest Hosts).

Escapees

Escapees RV Club is a support network for RVers.

Cost

- $39.95/annually
- $850 for lifetime

Benefits

- Support network with answers to basic RVer questions
- Travel guides
- Job center for finding work on the road
- Mail service & domicile options (additional fee)
- Rallies

The Problem with Escapees

I joined Escapees thinking that it was another RV park discount program. They do have some RV parks that offer Escapees members discounts, but Escapees is more about community and life on the road than about saving money. Escapees is a social club. If you're looking for another discount program, this is not the place to look.

Is Escapees worth it?

Finding community and connecting to other RVers on the road is not easy. We are often asked how to meet other RVers and how to combat loneliness on the road. Escapees offers meet-ups and rallies all across the country as a way to help connect RVers.

There are 11 rallies being hosted this month alone. Some of these rallies are free to attend as members while others may cost a fee. Plus, they have hundreds of articles and videos on their website to answer all of your RV-related questions–which is great for new RVers.

This is especially helpful when it comes to needing quick maintenance advice you can trust. If you are new to RVing, Escapees is a great membership for helping you If you are new to RVing, Escapees is a great membership for helping you learn more about the ins and outs of RVing and connect with other full-timers.

Plus, they also have "Xscapers" for younguns like Heath and me. If you're a "young" RVer (basically if you're under 50, you're young) then this is another great way to meet RVers who are not retirees. No offense retirees, but it's nice to meet working-age RVers too.

Thousand Trails

Thousand Trails offers a slightly different kind of membership club. For a larger upfront fee, you can camp without charge for up to 14 or 30 days at a time (depending on the level of membership you purchase) at participating Thousand Trails campgrounds.

Cost

- "$545 annually" (Quotation marks here because Thousand Trails pricing plans are more confusing than American healthcare)

Benefits

- 86 campgrounds in five "zones" across the country
- "Free" camping in your selected zone

The Problem with Thousand Trails

You either love or hate Thousand Trails. There is no in-between. I've heard they can be confusing and difficult, with horrible customer service. Not to mention that they are pricey, come with hefty restrictions, and figuring out which parks allow you to stay for free on which days can be a headache.

For a few years, Thousand Trails parks also had a reputation as being a little rundown. In 2017 we met a few members of the PR team at Equity Lifestyle Properties, the company that owns Thousand Trails and Encore Resorts. They let us know they are in the process of renovating and updating many of their parks to make them better destinations.

We visited three of their parks during a visit to the Florida Keys and they were all amazing. Hopefully this means that the brand is improving as a whole and will be a better deal for RVers in the future.

Is Thousand Trails worth it?

For some, yes. I know families who say they have saved thousands on lodging fees with TT. For others, no. I have friends who asked for a refund after a month because For others, no. I have friends who asked for a refund after a month because they had such terrible experiences at every park they visited.

The idea behind Thousand Trails is awesome. You pay an annual fee, you can stay at their locations for free all year, you save thousands of dollars on lodging and save time researching campgrounds. But it's kind of hit or miss. For us, the negative reviews have scared us away from joining the membership because the upfront investment is so high. If you do want to try Thousand Trails, the rumor is you should buy a used membership on eBay instead of paying full-price through Thousand Trails.

The Difference Between Trailer Parks, RV Parks, and Campgrounds

"There's a difference between RV parks and trailer parks." When you tell someone for the first time that you live in an RV, you see this flicker of recognition flash across a person's face as if the words "trailer trash" just bounced into their head. There is a HUGE difference between RV parks and trailer parks, and then there are campgrounds, which can encompass a wide range of amenities. So let's break down what each of these parks look like and what makes them different.

Trailer Parks

Trailer parks are for people who live in their RV (or mobile home) full-time. There is an important distinction here between people who live in RVs full-time and full-time RVers. Full-time RVers travel. People who live in RVs full-time stay in one place, often for years.

Trailer parks are filled with trailers and fifth wheels (and very rarely motorhomes), but also tend to include mobile homes and more permanent structures, since residents are long term.

This means they most likely don't accept overnight campers. There is a stigma that comes with trailer parks and unfortunately, this is what many people think about when they picture full-time RVing.

In fact, a friend told us that our lifestyle opened her mind to the idea of buying an RV to travel. "But I wouldn't want to be camping in those gross trailer parks," she said as her number one deterrent for RV life. Odds are, if you're full-time, you won't be staying in trailer parks. Sure, not every RV park is the nicest place I've ever slept, but most of them are safe, clean, and sometimes extremely awesome.

RV Parks

Much like hotels, RV parks have one major target audience: vacationers. This is why it's so incredibly frustrating to find an RV park in the summer. Every nuclear American family is out traveling the countryside in a Cruise America rental RV. Since there's something like 10,000 privately owned RV parks in the country, to make things simple I've broken down RV parks into three categories: off-theinterstate, standard, and resort.

Off-the-interstate and Long-term RV parks

These are going to be your cheapest and least desirable parks. These parks typically are more focused on being in a convenient location and giving you a decent rate than being a fun place to hang out for a weekend. For that reason, most RV parks you see right off the highway fall into this category.

(These are often your Good Sam and Passport America parks too.) We've stayed at a lot of convenient off-the-interstate style parks and they are just okay. These are great for cheap overnight stays when you're passing through an area, but aren't destinations where you want to spend any length of time, even if they do only cost $15/night.

RV parks designed for long-term guests often give us the same vibes. Longterm campers tend to store a lot of, well, junk outside their RV. We ended up at one these parks recently and our neighbors had a refrigerator, a plastic toy slide, a broken chair, and a whole heap of other untouched items sitting outside in between our sites. It definitely kills the "let's hang out by the campfire" vibes when you're looking at someone else's garbage. But it was close to the interstate and an easy place to stop for the night. It's worth noting that there are great RV parks for long-term guests, however, you aren't going to find them right off the interstate.

Most standard RV parks offer long-term camping options, but those parks will have higher standards for what your site can look like. These RV parks are good for inexpensive camping or you're just passing through an area, but we try to avoid these parks.

Standard RV Parks

Your standard RV park is going to be great for stays that last a weekend up to a month. These parks are going to be a little more expensive and will have a few more amenities on site. At a standard RV park, you can count on a nightly rate from $35-$50 and basic amenities like full hookup sites, internet access, and showers. But as a step higher than your cheap, off-the-interstate parks, they will typically offer at least one amenity to make their park more attractive.

Once in Virginia, I stayed at an RV park that offered free breakfast. A park in Wisconsin had a man-made lake filled with water slides, floating trampolines, and enough pool toys to occupy kids (or two fully grown adults like ourselves) for hours. Sometimes these parks are waterfront, on rivers, lakes, and ponds. You can count on these parks to be clean, well-kept, and generally focused on attracting vacationers, families, and retirees. This is the most common type of campground, so odds are as you're searching for campgrounds on the road, most will fall under this category.

Campgrounds

County park, state park, national park—these are typically where you find your campgrounds. Campgrounds encompass a wide range of possible amenities but they all agree on one thing: the whole point is to be in nature.

Whereas you will find RV parks in cities, off highways, and in more populated areas, campgrounds are usually reserved for the great outdoors. RV parks will often brand themselves as campgrounds if they offer cabins and tent sites in addition to RV camping. (But make no mistake, these places are really just your standard RV parks.)

Campgrounds—namely state and national park campgrounds—may or may not offer hookups. I would say that you have a 50/50 shot of having electrical and water hookups and very low chances of having sewage hookups. You will also not have amenities like wifi or pools, and there may not be showers available. But if you're at a campground, you probably don't want those things.

Well, you may want a shower. The point of campgrounds is to be close to wildlife, hiking, kayaking, and adventure. When we visit national parks, we always try to camp in the park campgrounds for this reason.

Choosing your Campsite

I'll get more into how to find RV parks and campgrounds in the next chapter. But what's important to think about is what type of camping you want to do on the road. If you're on a tight budget and plan on staying in one place, you might stay in a trailer park. If you're outdoorsy and want to explore national and state parks, then look for campgrounds. And if you're like me and you want A/C and the ability to shower daily, find a good RV park.

Supplement Your Income

Working on the Road

Today larger numbers of retirees are working well into their 60's and 70's. This trend is expected to continue. Retirement isn't what it used to be. People who opt for RVing during their retirement years will find many job opportunities out there. Typically, retirees who work while RVing are doing so to supplement their income. Consequently, their jobs on the road are part-time or contract opportunities that rarely include health insurance benefits. For the most part, retirees look for jobs that will provide what's commonly referred to as "walking around money." The choice comes down to what do you want to do and how much do you want or need to make.

There are also many (mostly younger) people living and working on the road who are not retired. These folks need to be employed in positions that will pay enough to be their primary source of income. More often than not they seek full time jobs with benefits. However, since this book is written specifically for retirees and near-retirees, the employment opportunities discussed here focus on the positions usually filled by retired persons.

Employment opportunities for RVing retirees generally fall into three broad categories:

1) Jobs where you stay in one location for specific lengths of time.

2) Jobs where you move from place to place in order to work.

3) Jobs that can be done anywhere, while on the move or in a single location.

More information in my previous book: **Rv Passive Income Guide: Top 10 Jobs That Can Be Done from Anywhere by Living your Full-Time RVing Nomad Life. Online Ideas and Advices for Aggressive Retirement and Beginners. Financial Freedom.**

https://www.amazon.com/dp/B095GL6ZHF

Seasonal Work

Among the major job sources for RV retirees are campgrounds, RV parks and RV resorts. They can be either federal/state/county-operated or privately-owned facilities. They all need to hire temporary or seasonal workers to supplement their permanent year-round staff. Work camping is one of the fastest growing trends in the job market in the U.S.

The most popular position is that of campground host at a federal, state or county park. Camper host jobs generally require a total of 20 hours work per week in return for a free campsite for whatever period of time is agreed upon…a month or two or a season. The hours are filled by a single individual or by a couple.

Among the tasks that may be required of the campground host(s) are greeting campers, registrations, assisting with finding and parking on the site, raking and cleaning camp sites and cleaning showers and rest rooms. These jobs are referred to as "volunteer" positions when there is no monetary salary included with the contract.

Retirees are attracted to campground host jobs because it gives them an opportunity to stay free for extended periods of time in some of the country's most scenic places, with plenty of leisure time to relax and enjoy the outdoor activities. Privately-owned campgrounds and resorts also have host positions. They give the free campsite for 20 hours work per week and, further, pay an hourly salary for additional hours worked.

Other part time and full time positions available at campgrounds and RV resorts include: activities director, fishing guides, tour guides, registration and gift shop clerks, maintenance workers, management positions, security, food services, shuttle bus drivers, gatekeepers, food service staff and others.

The advantage of working in campgrounds is that there are campgrounds and RV parks all over the country. Thus RVers have their choice of locale and can vary their work locations season by season. Many employers – campgrounds and RV resorts – prefer to hire people who bring their own housing with them.

Older workers are more dependable and when they live so close to the job, they're rarely late for work! When you apply for a position as campground host, don't be surprised if the employer asks for a photo of you and your rig with the application. Upscale resorts in particular want only clean and well-maintained (not necessarily brand new) rigs on their property.

The condition of your rig says something about you…it tips off a prospective employer about your work habits. Part time and full time seasonal jobs can be found at church camps, scout camps and camps for families of active and retired military. There are positions at amusement and theme parks, camping stores and seasonal resorts throughout the country.

Compensation varies broadly. Even when you secure a position that pays an hourly wage or weekly salary, a free site is usually part of the package. Some RVers manage to negotiate good compensation through a combination of wages and perks such as free site, free propane, free use of the laundry or tickets to local attractions.

There are so many positions available, job seekers can be selective. Snow birds who spend five or six months in a single sunny location can find seasonal jobs at many local establishments whose businesses increase during the season. Snow birds take jobs at retail stores, golf courses, restaurants, recreational facilities, tourist attractions and other places where the length of the employment contract *exactly* matches their time in the sunny locale.

Workers Moving Around

The classic job for those who like to travel around is RV delivery. Manufacturers hire drivers to deliver RVs from the factory to the dealer and dealers frequently hire drivers to take rigs to and from shows and rallies.

Other popular jobs for RVers include the wagonmaster, tailgunner and technical positions in RV caravans. Enterprising vendors carve out an income selling products that are of interest and value to RVers at local, state and national rallies and conventions sponsored by RV Clubs.

Many vendors also follow the RVIA show circuit offering their products to the thousands of people who attend the shows sponsored by RV manufacturers. Others, particularly artisans, artists and crafters, sell their wares at flea markets, fairs and (the granddaddy of 'em all) the annual "swap meet" during the winter season in Quartzsite, AZ.

Other RVing jobs that require individuals to travel around include sales for campground advertising, campground inspectors and representatives for corporations that do business with RV parks, RVers and the RV industry. Musicians, stand-up comedians and other performers are in demand for gigs at RV club rallies. Some traveling preachers and musicians can go from church to church and get to see the country during the week.

Jobs Anywhere You Are

Resourceful RV retirees can always devise ways to make some extra income doing what they've done all their lives. Hair stylists, barbers, RV technicians, auto mechanics, massage therapists and tailors can all provide their professional services on an as-needed basis wherever they happen to be.

Other services that can be marketed around the campground (with authorization from management) include RV washing, waxing and detailing and maintenance work.

Entrepreneurial RV retirees often identify a need and develop products or services on the road that keep them challenged and make some extra money as well. Some travelers who do not want to be tied down for a seasonal commitment will ask when they check into a campground if they need temporary help.

This is an especially effective approach for people who have handyman or clerical skills and for tradesmen with specific skills such as electrician, carpenter, computers, etc. RVers have been known to pick up "walking around money" this way…obtaining temporary work spontaneously. We know of a person who does very well as a windshield chip repair person.

All it took was a sign on the motor home advertising his skills at repairing windshield chips and his customers come to him. The computer aboard most RVs opens an array of jobs that can be done anywhere. These include consulting, technical writing, creative writing and illustrating, investments, business consulting and special projects, to name a few.

How to Find the Jobs

Employment positions discussed in this chapter are just a small portion of the jobs being filled by RV retirees. They are examples of the thousands of jobs that become available continuously nationwide. How do you learn about them? The Internet is the primary source. Employment ads also appear in the classified sections of RV magazines. Snow birds can use their local newspaper's employment classifieds as a source in their seasonal location.

The Workamper website is the largest employment service for RV travelers. It charges an annual membership fee and matches RVers with employers and visa versa. Founded in 1987, its publication, Workamper News is available in print and online. They also offer daily hotline job notifications and resume service.

Workamper sponsors job fairs that attract RVers who want to work and employers who want to hire them. A leading employer of campers is Recreation Resource Management, a private company that operates campgrounds and other recreational facilities in national forests and state parks. It manages some 175 sites in 11 states. The company maintains a work camping website – www.camphost.org – where persons seeking campground host positions may obtain information and complete an online application.

Work Opportunities

- www.workamper.com Brings job seekers and employers together.
- www.work-camping.com Work camping jobs at Recreation Resource Management areas.
- www.camphost.org Information about becoming a campground host at Recreation Resource Management areas.
- www.nps.gov/personnel This site is designed to provide basic information on career opportunities with the National Park Service. www.fs.fed.us/fsjobs Temporary employment opportunities with the U.S. Forest Service.
- www.yellowstonejobs.com Yellowstone National Park employment site.
- www.nps.gov/yose/jobs/ Yosemite National Park employment options.
- www.workatkoa.com Job opportunities at KOA Campgrounds.
- www.workersonwheels.com Jobs and resources for full-timers, work campers, and other RVers.

More information in my previous book: **Rv Passive Income Guide: Top 10 Jobs That Can Be Done from Anywhere by Living your Full-Time RVing Nomad Life. Online Ideas and Advices for Aggressive Retirement and Beginners. Financial Freedom.**

https://www.amazon.com/dp/B095GL6ZHF

Rules for boondocking

Below are some rules (written and unwritten) that apply to most boondocking locations. Be sure to follow these rules. Of course, these don't all apply in BLM areas.

- Ask the manager for permission.
- Don't put your leveling jacks down.
- Don't put the slides out (maybe just a little bit).
- Don't put the awnings out. Don't put lawn chairs out.
- Don't pull your grill out and start cooking.
- Don't run your generator (sometimes this is OK, particularly at truck stops).

In other words, you are 'parking' and not really 'camping.' It's not actually required, but for common courtesy reasons try to buy things from the business while you're parked in their parking lot—things such as gas, groceries, supplies, etc.

Since you're going to be buying these things anyway, why not buy from the businesses that are being nice to you? Bottom line: Boondocking is a great way for RVers to save a lot of money. Mix some boondocking in with your stays at campgrounds and your monthly campsite expenses can be cut way down. That puts more money in the budget for gas.

Planning for the Leap into Full-Time RVing

You need to do a little bit of planning before you embark on the full-time RV lifestyle, but it shouldn't take forever. I know people who have spent two or three years planning and trying to decide if they should venture out and try RVing full time. If you have two or three years before you can retire, it's OK to take that much time to do your research, but there's nothing you can do in two years that you can't do in two months—maybe with the exception of selling your house.

Choose this life not to escape life, but so that life doesn't escape you.

There will always be unknowns and as Yogi Berra said, "It's tough to make predictions, especially about the future." There's one other important thing to do and that is to be sure to actually listen when you're discussing this with your spouse. Make sure it's something you both want to do. If one of you wants to do it and the other one is reluctantly going along with the idea, it may not work.

On the other hand, I have seen couples where one person wasn't really excited about the idea, but after getting on the road, the reluctant one really got into it and was gung-ho. I have had several people tell me that their plan was to do it for a year or two, but after they got into the lifestyle, they didn't want to go back to a 'normal' life.

And I've seen it go the other way too. There are lots of ways you can go about getting ready to hit the road. I know of one couple who bought their motorhome a year before they retired. They moved into it and lived in a nearby RV park for the year. This allowed them to get used to the idea. They packed and repacked their RV and made some modifications to it. This gave them time to get rid of all of their stuff. They also put their house on the market and sold it during the year. The day he retired, they literally pulled out of the RV park and hit the road.

To make your dream come true of someday living life as a full-time RVer, there are a lot of things that have to be done. Everything has to fall (or be pushed) into place to make your RV lifestyle a reality. There are so many things that you have to do or make decisions about that it's hard to even know where to start.

To make it happen, set a date

As long as you plan to live the RV life someday, it will never happen. The time will never be just perfect. The best way to make your dream a reality is to set a date. Set a date that's realistic, but ambitious. After you set a date, mark it on your calendar, tell your family and friends. It's no longer a dream, it's a matter of fact. Consider throwing a going away party for yourselves. This will make the fact that you really are going to hit the road on your announced date firmer.

Next, start making things happen.

For most people, the biggest obstacle is getting rid of their house. Take steps to solve this problem first. Call a real estate agent and get your house on the market to sell or rent. Don't sit idle and wait for the house to sell. You've already set a date that you're going to hit the road. Get busy taking care of the other things that must be done. A word about selling your house—I've seen people have their houses on the market for two or three years before there was a sale. A lot of people have an unrealistic expectation about what their house is worth. Don't fall into that trap. It's worth what it will sell for now.

The main reason a house doesn't sell is that the owner has set an unrealistic price. Set your price at a fair market value (or maybe a little less) and your house will sell. I've heard people say that they're going to wait for the housing market to rebound. If you really thought housing prices were going to go up 15% to 20% within the next year, wouldn't you be buying real estate like mad? Put your house on the market, set a fair price and if it doesn't sell within a reasonable time, lower the price and keep doing this until it sells or until you decide to keep the house and rent it out.

At that point, get it rented. My neighbor had her place on the market for over a year and then finally sold it for less than she had turned down a month after it was listed. Your house is worth what it will sell for now—not what you think it's worth and not what it was worth a few years ago. My mother and father sold their house (and a lot of the stuff inside the house) at an auction after they moved into a condo.

Maybe you're not that brave, but a good auction company will get a fair price for your house. I'm not recommending that you have an auction to sell your house, but if all else fails, it's an option. While your house is on the market, get rid of all of your stuff that you don't need—which will be almost everything.

See the next chapter on how to get rid of your stuff. It's easier than you think. If you don't have a deadline, you will never get to the end of your to-do list. Not everything that you would like to get done has to be done before you hit the road. You are not like Lewis and Clark heading off into the wilderness for two years. You can do things while you're on the road. For example, I recommend that you get your banking set up with two banks that have branches nationwide.

It would be nice if this was taken care of before you left, but you can do it while you're on the road. You may want a better (or a lower priced) car to tow behind your motorhome. You can sell your present car and then buy something else while you're on the road. Concentrate on taking care of the things that absolutely must to be taken care of before you leave.

Remember, you have a departure date. If you didn't get your riding lawnmower sold, give it to someone. You'll be surprised how fast things happen when you really do have a firm departure date. Once you've made the decision to try full-time RVing, don't waste time second guessing yourself. Six months or a year or two down the road you can reevaluate the situation and if being a full-time RVer isn't making you happy, you can sell your RV and buy or rent a house or condo and live wherever you wish. You're not locked permanently into your decision. The important thing is to make a decision.

It's OK to make a decision to not embark on living full time in an RV, but in my opinion, it's not OK to not make a decision. When you're sitting in a rocking chair on the front porch of a nursing home, it's OK to say, "I thought about living full time in an RV at one time, but I decided not to do it." It's not OK to say, "I thought about living full time in an RV at one time, but I never got around to doing it."

Other costs associated with living full time in an RV

The fee for campsites can be a major expense and can vary from quite high to very reasonable or even to zero when you're boondocking. Boondocking is a term used to describe camping where it's free, but where there is no water, electricity or sewer hookups. We'll talk more about boondocking in a later chapter.

Here are some typical numbers to think about. Campsite fees range from about $18 a night to $45, with $20 to $30 being about typical for a single night.

Another option is to book a camping space for a month or more at at time. You can stay in some very nice campgrounds for $300 to $450 a month. This includes electricity, WiFi, water, sewer, trash pickup and sometimes cable TV is included. Monthly rates run about two times the weekly rate, so whether you stay for two weeks or for a month, the cost will be about the same. Also, by staying a month you get to relax, meet people, see the sights, and enjoy what the local area has to offer.

There are ways to get discounts. For example, if you join *PassPortAmerica.com* for $45 a year, you can stay in thousands of participating campsites for half price. As you might expect, some conditions apply. You can join *Escapees.com* and get discounts too.

To cut expenses while they're traveling, a common practice of RVers is to stay in a campsite for about $24 for one night and then stop and boondock two nights in Walmart parking lots along their way. That means that they spent a total of $24 for three nights of camping or $8 a night. Of course, if you stay three nights in Walmart parking lots and one night in a campground, you will get the average price down to $6 a night. Not all Walmarts will allow you to park overnight, but most will. Be sure to check with the manager and get permission before you spend the night.

If you're traveling and just making miles, stopping at Walmart parking lots two or three nights in a row and then getting up and hitting the road again each morning is a great way to cover a lot of miles with minimum campground fees.

Also, since you're not putting down leveling jacks, extending the slide-outs, hooking up water, electric, and sewer, there's nothing to do the next morning except start your engine and hit the road. But be sure to crank your TV antenna down if you cranked it up the night before. One easy way to remember to do this is to hang your ignition key on the antenna crank handle.

More information in my previous book: **Rv Passive Income Guide: Top 10 Jobs That Can Be Done from Anywhere by Living your Full-Time RVing Nomad Life. Online Ideas and Advices for Aggressive Retirement and Beginners. Financial Freedom.**

https://www.amazon.com/dp/B095GL6ZHF

What about the cost of gasoline or diesel fuel?

Everyone thinks that the cost of fuel is a major expense with an RV and it is if you travel almost every day or travel back and forth across the country — and some people do.
But if you stay in one campground for a month and then travel 300 miles to another one, this would add up to 3,600 miles a year. As we discussed earlier, this is about average for most people who are full-time RVers.
Let's do the math. Assume that you drive 3,600 miles a year and are getting nine miles per gallon. Some RVs get 8 mpg or less and some get 10 mpg or more. How fast you drive and what kind of rig you have will affect your mileage, but these numbers are in the ballpark.
That would mean that you would use 400 gallons of gas a year and at $3.50 a gallon, that would be $1,400 a year for gas or $117 a month. You're probably spending more than $117 a month on gas now in your present lifestyle. What if you drive twice the national average and drive 7,000 miles a year, that's still only $234 a month for gas.
As you can see from the above analysis, the cost of gas is not really an issue. It comes down to which lifestyle you would enjoy the most — the RV lifestyle or your conventional stick and brick lifestyle.
By doing a little research you will be better informed and able to recognize a good deal when you start physically looking at RVs. Keep in mind that there will be some maintenance expenses with any RV. Most of the time it will be nothing major. The engines run forever. You will need new tires every five to seven years.
By the way, when looking at tires, you can't go by the tread. You will have to go by the date code (which I will explain in a later chapter). Almost all motorhomes will have tires with good treads. With your stick and brick house you will have maintenance expenses, such as $5,000 for a new roof, $6,000 for a new heat pump or air conditioner, etc.

Your RV probably won't have maintenance expenses that high, but do budget $1,000 or so a year depending on the age of your rig, how much you travel and, of course, a diesel(also called a DP for diesel pusher), will be more expensive to maintain. A lot of the things you spend money on will not be something that has to be done—at least, not immediately—things like new carpet, reupholstering the couch, etc. One of the things that make the RVing lifestyle so affordable is that you have a lot of control over how much you spend each month and you can change it in a heartbeat. When you live the conventional lifestyle, you don't have many options to change your monthly living expenses.

For example, if you have expensive repair work that needs done on your rig this month, you can almost totally eliminate fuel cost, by not traveling. You can also almost (if not entirely) eliminate camping fees by boondocking on public lands, in Walmart parking lots (only one or two nights at a time) or by doing some volunteer work at a state or national park campground in exchange for free camping. You can also do what is called workamping for a month or so and get free camping.

You can find out more about workamping at *WorKamping.com* and I will talk more about it in the chapter on, "Ways to Make Money Without a Computer." In a nutshell, workamping is where you get free camping in exchange for working a few hours a week. Sometimes there is a small salary paid also.

You can buy your first RV very inexpensively. Trade up later if you want to when you know more about what you want. When you get to the chapter about "How Much Will an RV Cost?", you will see just how much RV you can get for very little money.

Your monthly living expenses (assuming you are not paying off debt or making payments on a car or RV) can vary from less than $1,000 to over $3,000 a month depending on how much you travel, how much you eat out, and other personal and entertainment expenses you choose to make. This amount includes campsite rental with water, electricity, sewer, WiFi, and cable TV. It also includes food, insurance, an allowance for some maintenance, and some gas. You can get this amount even lower by boondocking some and/or doing volunteer work in exchange for free camping.

Of course, you can spend a lot more.

Bottom line: I think after reading this chapter you will agree that, "Yes, you can afford to live full time in your RV." Now let's go on and look at some more information to help you decide if living the RV lifestyle is what you want to do.

Digital communications from the RV

Smartphones

For full-timers, the cellular phone is the home phone and the only phone number(s) you have. When the land line gets disconnected give the cell phone number as the new number on the recorded message that runs for 30 days afterward. Wireless phone service is available throughout the country, and since you'll be traveling to many area codes, you will want to use a company with consistent nationwide service – currently AT&T Wireless and Verizon are regarded as the carriers with best overall coverage.
Both have retail and online stores where you can consult with a technician to set up a plan for your unique RVing needs and budget. Use the store locator feature on the company's website to find a location where you can actually go in and meet personally with a technician to design your cellular plan. NOTE: Be sure to verify that it is a company-owned store, as that's where you will find the knowledgeable service personnel.

- *Satellite*: This is the technology that works virtually everywhere as long as the satellite dish has an unobstructed view of the southern sky (don't park under a tree). However, there are longer delays with a satellite Internet connection, and it is the most expensive of the three methods listed here.
- *Wi-Fi Hot Spots*: Networks are installed at many campgrounds and public Wi-Fi hot spots can also be found at libraries and coffee shops. Some are free and some charge a user fee. When you are using a hot spot, you are sharing the Internet service at that location with other users, so data security of e-mail communications can be an issue. When using a shared network you need to be within range of the host.

TV In The RV

Nearly every RV has a TV (or two) as part of the standard furnishings. All you need to do is decide what type of TV service you'll use. If you add a satellite dish—there are two basic styles: push-button rooftop or manual on a tripod—you can subscribe to the hundreds of channels available through one of two major satellite TV companies. The company provides the receiver (as well as the monthly bill). If you don't want to invest in the satellite equipment, most campgrounds have a cable TV hookup at the site and it's generally included in the camping fee. You will also be able to get local channels in most locations free.

You Too Can Be A Savvy Digital Consumer

The preceding section contains a brief, bare-bones outline of the electronic communications currently available for today's RVers. Just 20 years ago, they wouldn't have been possible. If you are "technically challenged," like I am, you might be somewhat overwhelmed by this section. Today's retirees did not grow up in the digital age…the bits, bytes, kilobytes, and so on seem like a foreign language to us. When I purchased my first "smart" phone, I quickly discovered that I wasn't "smart" enough to teach myself how to use it, and my 11-year-old granddaughter, Megan, became my best teacher. Before you decide which electronic devices you want to have onboard your RV, gather information, troll the RV forums for facts and opinions, use the Internet resources listed at the end of this chapter and ask other RVers about the communications they use. Before you purchase electronic equipment and digital devices, discuss your situation with a technician. Ask a lot of questions. We found that the younger techs usually have a better grasp of digital electronics. You're not going to become a geek overnight, but you definitely need to determine which electronic devices will suit your needs and budget. Do your research and become an educated consumer who will ultimately make wise decisions.

Important Papers and Valuables

Our house on wheels doesn't have a security system like our stick-built house did. Although the RV is reasonably safe and secure whether on the road or parked, accidents do happen. A concern we had about being on the road full time was that our children would have access to information they would need in the event of a common disaster. Important papers are not as secure traveling around in an RV as they would be, for instance, in a stationary metal box on the shelf of the bedroom closet. Our solution was to rent a bank safe deposit box for storing important papers and valuables. Another option is to place the important papers in a fire-proof metal box and leave them with a family member or trusted friend. Either way, the originals of your vital documents won't be at risk by dragging them all over the country. You may also want to consider placing valuable jewelry in the safe box.

Before going on the road we sorted through and carefully organized all our financial records and important papers. This was another good result that came out of the preparations to go full-time. Organizing and updating records is a chore people tend to put off…and we're no different. Plowing through all the paper, we found duplicates and outdated stuff that could be put through the shredder. When the tasks were finished, we had a well-organized stack of vital records including: wills and durable powers of attorney, life insurance and annuity contracts, birth and marriage certificates, cemetery deed, stock certificates, savings bonds, documentation of current accounts and their financial institutions, property deed and military records. Most are now in the safe deposit box.

However, there are certain documents you'll need to keep in the RV or in the car. These include vehicle registrations and insurance documentation for both the motor home and dinghy or the truck and trailer. Also, we carry our passports in case we decide to go out of the country…and we have the vehicle titles with us in case we decide to replace either vehicle. These important originals are kept in the rig in a small fireproof box.

If you have a computer on board, you may want to scan all your important papers and burn the copies to a CD. It is a time-consuming process the first time, but updates (where applicable) won't take as long. There are software packages available to help you manage this process.

Medical Care and Prescription Drugs

Medical care and medical insurance coverage is always an important issue, but it takes on added significance as we move into retirement years. We've learned, since going on the road, that every individual is responsible to know all about their health records and be fully apprised of any medical conditions. Furthermore, we are responsible to keep ourselves in good shape – physically and mentally. In the long run, that's the best medical care.

Before you hit the road, have a general physical checkup from your current physician and, while you're there, ask for copies of all relevant medical records. It's a good idea to carry these documents with you. However, even though we've had several occasions when we needed to get emergency treatment at hospital emergency rooms and routine consultations at doctor's offices or walk-in clinics, not once did they ask for medical records. The first thing they want is proof of insurance. In one place I offered to bring my medical records and was told they prefer to do their own testing and diagnosis because health conditions change. And that made sense. However, they always asked for a record of all medications we're currently taking and, of course, proof of insurance.

This segues to the next topic: prescription drugs. If you have not already done so, take the time to make a list of all medications and doses (including vitamins) that you currently take. It is a sure sign of aging when you need to buy one of those little plastic boxes with S-M-T-W-T-F-S on top. You know the ones I'm talking about…the box that, in my younger days, I said I'd never need. Well, I need it now! The list of my medications and doses is taped to the inside cover of the plastic box, just to be sure I don't misplace the list.

Before you leave your land-locked domicile, have your prescriptions filled at a pharmacy that has a nationwide network. Once you're in their computer system you'll be able to have prescriptions filled with ease anywhere in the country. Check the number of refills the prescribing physician has authorized. Often the prescription is only good for 6 or 12 refills and then the doctor wants to see you to monitor whether you still need that medication and at that dosage. If and when this occurs you would need to decide whether you want to return to your previous doctor for an annual checkup, or find another doctor for a periodic checkup.

What if a problem arises and one of us needs to have surgery or go into a hospital for some other inpatient treatment? Believe it or not, living full-time in an RV is advantageous in such a situation. Have you ever seen a motor home or fifth wheel parked in a hospital lot with the jacks down? It's likely that an individual is in the hospital and the spouse is staying in the lot. Or, when the hospital stay is longer than a few days the spouse could pull into a nearby campground and hookup for the duration of the hospitalization.

Check your medical insurance plan(s) to determine procedures to be followed for obtaining routine medical care and in emergency situations. Most insurers (including Medicare) will honor claims from participating providers throughout the country. However, if you are in an HMO, their procedures can vary; call the carrier, explain your situation and ask for advice. It is possible that you might need to change insurers when you become a full-time traveler. It's better to confirm up front that your coverage will be valid rather than find out later when you file a claim after you're on the road.

Staying Healthy on the Road

Every RVer should have good knowledge of First Aid. If you've never taken a basic First Aid course, now is the time to do it. After all, you're retired. Call the local YMCA, health department at city hall or the community school and find out where you can enroll. First Aid and basic CPR courses are offered at some RV rallies. First Aid kit items should always be in your RV's medicine cabinet.

We're often asked, "At what age will you have to stop full-timing?" Age is not the major factor, health is! Maintain healthy routines to keep yourself in good shape. Exercise regularly, and eat sensibly.

There is no good reason to avoid exercise on the road. You may not be able to keep up your membership at the gym and the RV doesn't have room for a treadmill, but you can walk every day, everywhere you go…and walking is an effective form of exercise. RVers get to walk in varied locales, giving them a chance to see and appreciate each region's unique beauty. Other kinds of exercise for RVers include cycling, dancing, swimming, tennis and golf. My husband is a golf nut…he's enjoyed the experience of different courses all over the country and has had the pleasure of meeting locals wherever we go. Walking is great sport. You never know when a walk will lead to a memorable experience. One time we were staying at a state park in Mississippi during off season. The weather was beautiful – mild, but not too hot – so I went on a long walk every day. A snow white beach on the Gulf was just across the street and there were woodsy areas around the park, so I was able to enjoy exploring both areas. One day I saw a path into the woods; a small wooden sign read "outdoor chapel." Out of curiosity I followed the path for half a mile or so when it opened on to a clearing that had a small set of wooden benches facing a rough hewn wooden altar. The trees formed a cathedral ceiling over the area. I sat on the bench for a long time, savoring the silence. And, alone in that quiet, hushed clearing in the woods, I felt the presence of God. I will long remember the feeling of serenity that washed over me that day in the little outdoor chapel in the Mississippi woods.

Storage Unit

At the beginning, I was unsure whether I would even like the RV lifestyle, much less enjoy doing it full time. Everything was entirely new and totally unfamiliar. I learned RVing by immersion. Going RVing full-time was a leap of faith for me. So, we made a commitment to try it for a year and we prepared for the possibility that we'd go back to a land-locked domicile.

Initially, the purpose of renting a storage unit was to keep some furniture to get us started should we move back into a house next year. One year flowed into two and then three and we continued to pay rent on the climate controlled storage unit. At the beginning of the fourth year, I calculated how much we had spent for renting the storage shed versus the approximate value of the "stuff" we had stored there. It was no longer worth it…especially now that my perspective had changed.

Material possessions are not that important anymore. A whole house full of beautiful furniture will never be as lovely as walking in the Redwood Forest…a wide screen TV will never be as spectacular as the sunset over the desert…having my own swimming pool would not ever compare to wading into the Pacific and Atlantic Oceans, the Gulf of Mexico, Lake Michigan and the Mississippi River all in the same year (not in that order). You'll not fully appreciate the spectacular natural beauty of this country by flying over it, nor will you appreciate all this country has to offer during quick two-week trips in the car. When I saw the Grand Canyon for the first time, I thought, "Now I've seen the most wondrous of my country's natural wonders." But that was just the beginning. Since then, I've been fortunate enough to see dozens more natural wonders. There has been so much more to see, savor and appreciate! Every day is a beautiful day of discovery.

After looking inside the storage unit, we wondered why in the world we kept all that stuff, and then proceeded to give it all away, including fairly new TVs that went to some nice young people. We got a lot more joy from the giving than they did from the getting. For the irreplaceable items such as family photos and heirlooms a small climate controlled storage unit, about the size of a large walk-in closet, works…and the cost is modest. Another option is to give those things to family members who are apt to inherit them someday anyway. At least you'll be around to see the treasured items being used.

The Choice Includes Some Trade-Offs

After several years as a full-time RVer, members of my family still struggle to comprehend the nomadic lifestyle. No one in the family has ever traveled in an RV. As a result, they are as unfamiliar with the lifestyle as I was when I first moved into our magnificent mobile home. My brother still asks if I've made up my mind about what I want to do when I grow up. When we were parked at a campground near their house, the grandchildren enjoyed coming to visit the RV. Granny's house on wheels, which resembles a large playhouse, is a hit with the kids. On the other side, their parents were a little concerned.

Traditionalists are unfamiliar with the lifestyle of full-time RVing. We weren't singing about grandmother's house on wheels when we sang "Over the river and through the woods, to grandmother's house we go." When grandmother travels frequently, she is referred to as a "gypsy," not as the grandmother in an apron whose home is constantly filled with the delightful aroma of freshly baked apple pie.

No matter how much the rig cost, full-timers suffer from the trailer-park-trash label in some aspects. Full-timing is extremely fulfilling, and it can lead to the happiest retirement years of our lives, but there are drawbacks. Children and grandkids do not "come home" to visit for holidays or to be gathered around the dining room table for Sunday supper for full-time RVing grandparents. Some RVing grandparents are fortunate enough to travel with their grandchildren on occasion. However, for many others whose families wish to preserve their distance from the "abnormal" lifestyle, it's only a pipe dream.
While the RV allows full-timers to see friends and family on a regular basis, they are always the ones who travel to see relatives and rarely have the opportunity to host people at their home. This is seen as a disadvantage by some. However, for a few of adventurous old(er) persons, full-time RVing is still the finest option to spend part or all of their retirement years. It's all about the journey!

You Can Go Home Again

When thinking about full-time RVing for retirement, most people instinctively know the day will come when they have to hang up the keys…and they worry about it. "Isn't it better to buy a small place now to have for the future?" they ask. Well sure, if you want to pay property taxes, utilities and maintenance on an empty place for however long you're on the road. (Refer back to Chapter 3.) Another approach might be to earmark part of the nest egg for future use and let it gain a reasonable rate of return during your full-timing years. Put the house in the bank, so to speak. Land-locked properties will always be on the market. Meanwhile you can enjoy freedom to explore all the states in this great land. And, if and when you're ready, you'll have a better idea of the next place you want to call home.

More information in my previous book: **Rv Passive Income Guide: Top 10 Jobs That Can Be Done from Anywhere by Living your Full-Time RVing Nomad Life. Online Ideas and Advices for Aggressive Retirement and Beginners. Financial Freedom.**

https://www.amazon.com/dp/B095GL6ZHF

Full-Timers Checklist

- Shop and research thoroughly before buying an RV.
- Sell the house.
- Decide what to do with furnishings and other "stuff" & disburse them.
- Rent storage unit if needed.
- Obtain insurance to cover the RV for full-time living.
- Prepare & pack the rig.
- Pick a home state; establish the new address.
- Change address on everything normally received in the mail.
- Review financial records & important papers.
- Decide where to store important papers & valuables.
- Arrange to have financial transactions done electronically.
- Confirm that current health insurance will cover full time travelers.
- Disconnect phone land line; use cell phone number as forward.
- Transition from desktop to laptop computer.
- Have medical checkup & get relevant medical records.
- Get current/new prescription(s).
- Arrange to have prescription(s) filled at national pharmacy.
- Make list of medications.
- Get pet's shots updated & obtain relevant records from vet.

On The Road

Do It Your Way

Go where you want, stay where you want, for as long as you want. That about sums it up. When you go RVing, you are in the driver's seat, literally and figuratively. The big day finally arrives, all the arrangements have been made and the trip is about to begin. So, how is it done?

The best answer is: do it your way…develop your own one-of-a-kind RV travel model as you go along. The RV lifestyle is learned only by actually doing it on the road.

Our first trip in the RV – the maiden voyage, so to speak – was going to be just a two-week jaunt within our home state, from Jacksonville to Key West, with one or perhaps two stops along the way.

I was hell-bent on a true nomadic existence. "Should we make reservations?" asked my husband, the driver, the night before we left.

"Don't be silly," said I, the co-pilot, (who, by the way, had no previous camping experience). "We'll find places to stay along the way." Well-armed with two huge campground directories (it was the "old days," before digital listings) I was confident. We drove for a few hours when I finally decided to crack open the brand new giant campground book. For a newbie, it was overwhelming! All those little marks on the map. Where are we now? What's the milepost? Where will we be when it's time to stop for the night? There was so much to cross reference, from the map to the listings…back 'n forth, back 'n forth. Before long I was taking notes furiously. Cities along the route, current milepost, milepost an hour from now.

Then I started with the questions: How many amps do we need? What's a central dump? Is typical site width 30' good for us? Are we a big rig? Why do they say heaters allowed? Finally, my driver (the experienced but exasperated camper) said, "Enough already! Just pick something, I'm tired!" I selected one listing and phoned them; yes, we have a couple of spots for tonight, just give us your name and credit card number. Armed with the hefty directory, I directed us to the campground, and thus successfully carried out my first co-pilot chore.

But, when we arrived, were we ever surprised! It was a classic "trailer park" – mostly permanent residents, and a couple of spaces near the back of the property for the rare overnighter who, like us, happened to venture in off the road. It seemed like every one of the residents came out of their trailers to watch us get our brand new rig settled into the spot next to the back fence. I tried to ignore the audience. "I'm tired, I don't care," muttered the driver as he plugged in the electric and hooked up the water. I'd like to say we had a restful first night in our new home, but we were backed into a site at the rear end of the property where only a chain link fence separated us from the railroad tracks. At least three freight trains whistled through during the night.

The next morning, we weight-lifted both campground directories onto the table, figured out how to navigate through them and made a few phone calls to south Florida. It was January, the height of the season in the south. We were able to find available space in the Keys, but just barely. We secured two nights at one RV park and three at another. And the nightly fees were much higher than we expected. So much for the anticipated week at the beach.

The first trip, our test run, wasn't a rousing success, but we sure did learn a lot. Even nomads have to be sensible, especially when they're in a 38-foot motor home with a toad. That behemoth can't randomly pull over and stay just anywhere for the night.

But, this is RVing…an adventure. After those first few days we were well on the way toward developing our own personal RV style. The major attraction to the RV experience is that it gives adventurous travelers a way to explore new places, soak up the unique environs of different parts of the country and meet the people who reflect the personality of the region. As retirees, you can go RVing state by state, region by region or destination to destination at your own pace.

In spite of the inauspicious beginning, we two happily traveled full-time for many years and developed a travel style that's comfortable and fun for us.

In our travels we've observed that RV travel styles can range from free spirit to groupies, and everything in between. But most people are a little of both styles.

"Free spirits" are classic happy wanderers, not too regimented. They enjoy being with people, but they also want to go off into the wilderness to enjoy hiking, fishing and just being with nature. Then they'll decide to go to a major city they've not seen before and take a guided tour. Generally the free spirits don't set schedules too far in advance. They are the ones who drive the family "back home" crazy. Usually, when free spirits call family, the first question is, "Where are you now?" Conversely, "groupies" join clubs, attend monthly group camp-outs and like to plan and arrange RV club events.

Very often they become club officers and actively recruit new members. They get involved in activities such as Volunteers on Wheels and Habitat for Humanity. Groupies like to travel in caravans. Some also supplement their incomes by leading caravans or by selling their wares at RV rallies. Unlike the free spirits, their schedules are set well in advance.

There is no specific plan of action for RV traveling. Traveling styles are as unique as the individuals and their rigs. Here are a few points (not necessarily in any logical order) that have enhanced our travel experiences:

- An informational stop per state. Whenever we cross a state line, we stop at the Welcome Center. There's a plethora of valuable information to be had at these places. Browsing the brochures will give you a feel for the personality of the state. Some travelers look specifically for museums, others zero in on historic sites, entertainment venues, tourist attractions, outdoor activities or state and federal parks. If you don't see what you're looking for, ask. Some centers file information about their state and county parks under the counter. Welcome Centers are a good resource for travelers and some of them even offer coffee and cookies.
- Don't push and tire yourself out. After a few weeks, you'll have enough experience to be able to establish a general guideline for how many hours/miles per day are suitable for you. Everyone has their own comfort level. Keep reminding yourself that you're retired now…no longer on the job; it will take some time to wind down.

- Be flexible. Our friends Carla and Skip started counting the days a full year before they retired. They were going to be extended travelers – not quite full-timing, but leaving their landlocked domicile behind for months at a time to go out and play. By the time the big day arrived, they had their first journey—three months in duration—thoroughly scheduled. About a week after they left, both came down with the flu. They were in Arkansas and had to hunker down at a campground for a few days longer than the one night that was on the carefully-crafted schedule. "My whole schedule is shot," Skip reported to us. "I had to make a dozen phone calls to cancel reservations along the way, and then figure out how we're going to make up the lost time." After we got that call from Skip, I thought about it. Did our friends really have to make up for "lost time?" It reminded me that, at our age, there is no such thing as "lost" time, just "more" time...time given to appreciate and enjoy being retired, even if it's a few extra nights in Arkansas sipping chicken soup.
- Avoid driving at night. Once we were driving on a main road in a remote part of the great state of Texas. It was getting to be mid-afternoon when I queried, "It looks like there's a nice campground coming up in a few miles. Want to stop there for tonight?" The pilot wasn't tired and felt like going another 50 miles or so. We breezed by the nice campground, not realizing it would be the last one for about 200 miles. It was dark, pitch black, when we finally pulled in for the night, tired and cranky. Another lesson learned. Remote areas can be tricky when it comes to finding places to stay. Stopping well before sunset is better than driving into the dark.
- Always drive defensively. This can never be emphasized enough. Be aware of the other drivers on the road; give them plenty of room when they're passing. Don't make any sudden, sharp moves. Always be aware of the size of the vehicle you're driving and the space required to pass, to make turns or to cut across lanes of traffic. If you miss an exit, keep going. Above all, don't speed. Seeing an RV accident is a sobering experience and, the first time you see one, it will reinforce all the aforementioned tips.
- Avoid peak times and days. A recent study identified the 10 deadliest days on the roadways of America: Jan. 1, July 2, 3 & 4, Aug. 3, 4, 6 & 12, Sept. 2 and Dec. 23. These days are all associated with holidays and/or vacation times. The day before Thanksgiving is also a hazardous day on the roads. One of the benefits of being a traveling retiree is we can avoid the heavy traffic times and days. Don't go out on

the roadways on days when it seems like the rest of the country is rushing to get somewhere for a holiday or a vacation. It is also wise to plan your drive times to steer clear of rush hours in major metropolitan areas.

- Watch the weather: Since we're on the road, the Weather Channel has become one of our favorite stations. Always check the weather on your travel route and in the general vicinity of your destination. Even though you wake up to a clear and sunny day, you could be surprised by inclement weather en route. Avoid high winds and driving in stormy weather. Keep yourselves informed about weather patterns. Remember, your home is on wheels. Consequently you're capable of outrunning a hurricane or getting out of the way of a tornado.

GPS (Global Positioning System)

GPS—the satellite-based navigational system—uses a network of 24 satellites in orbit to continuously transmit signal information to the earth. A GPS receiver uses that information to calculate the precise location of the receiver and create directions to any other location. This information is displayed on the GPS receiver's electronic map.

GPS is an essential navigation tool for RV travelers. It identifies your exact location (anywhere, at any given time) and it provides precise voice and on-screen directions from Point A to Point B; it can also give detour directions to avoid traffic problems, find the nearest gas stations, rest areas, shopping, restaurants, and much more. The places it can take you to are seemingly endless, as long as the coordinates, or even the street addresses, are in its data base.

Prices range from about $100 for an entry-level GPS to between $200-$400 for RV-specific devices. Cellular phones can be used as a GPS also. Generally, any GPS device can provide basic directions, but many go beyond the basics. RV-specific devices usually have a larger screen, the option to enter profile information for your rig (i.e., weight, height, length, etc.), an option to give the GPS verbal instructions rather than keying them in, identifies road hazards and, RV/truck routes and has detailed campground and RV park listings, locations of major attractions and landmarks and more.

Trip Planning

By now you probably have a general idea of where you want to go and the things you want to do once you hit the road. Planning the trip can be as exciting as taking the trip itself. Here are some key trip-planning tools:

- Free computerized map programs that will calculate routes (quickest, shortest, most scenic, etc.) to a destination or series of destinations. Rather than using the GPS for mapping, you may want to pull up one of those programs onto the lap top so you'll have the benefit of a wider screen as well as a note pad beside you as you consider different routes and destinations.
- RV travel books and Internet sites about specific areas of the country and popular destinations. You can find websites dedicated to everything from scenic drives to amenities along the interstates as well as places to find free overnight parking. Informative books geared specifically to campers are available to help you find a variety of places from national parks and state parks to casinos, factory tours, popular attractions and even the very-necessary dump stations. Purchasing a book that narrows the field to your particular interest can save you many frustrating hours of surfing the net. RV bookstores online and in specialty stores such as Camping World have the books for RV travelers.
- Traditional atlas—the big paperback one that's been a staple in every vehicle since 1954— is still being used. RV-copilots still want to have the state-by-state map in the lap. There are times in every traveler's day when they need to reach for a specialty book instead of an electronic device.

Places To Go / Things To See

One thing is certain about America The Beautiful – it's big! So much to see…so many great places to discover. The U.S. Interstate Highway System is unique – there's nothing like it in the world. Most of your RV driving will be done on the 46,000+ miles of efficient, generally wellmaintained and mostly free interstates. And, at other times, you'll also get to experience the charm of other highways and byways.

Places waiting for you out there include:

- Public Lands
- The 49th State
- Historic Sites and Museums
- Cities, Towns and Waterways

Public Lands: Recreational activities abound at national parks and forests, along the nation's waterways and in the mountains. Camping on public lands puts you right where the action is! However, larger sites with hookups are not available in all areas, especially wilderness and forest preserves. Reservations for big rig campsites should be made well in advance, especially during peak tourist seasons. The 12 national parks that form the sweeping "grand circle" from Utah to Arizona and Colorado are especially popular, as are Yellowstone and Yosemite. Excellent camping, fishing and water sports can be found at Corps of Engineers-managed campgrounds. Spectacular monuments such as Mount Rushmore are also waiting along the way.

The 49th State: Alaska is a perennial RV destination. Noted for its unique scenic beauty, incredible vistas and abundant wildlife, Alaska is such a huge state, it's virtually impossible to take it all in on just a single trip. Clearly, fishing and sightseeing are the most common attractions. The scope of the trip is awesome, so do extensive planning and allow plenty of time to make it worthwhile. RV caravans to Alaska are popular, and may be worth considering for the first trip. However, going it alone allows time to linger along the way, find your own fishing places and take side trips on your own schedule.

Historic Sites and Museums: The oldest city in the U.S. is in Florida, the cradle of Liberty is in Massachusetts and the most-visited presidential library is in California. History comes alive at Williamsburg, Plymouth and in mining towns throughout the west. Indian traditions are celebrated in the Navajo Nation. We've been to a dinosaur museum in Colorado and the Spam museum, in Minnesota. Our wanderings allowed us to find lots of interesting, albeit littleknown, museums and historic spots. Be curious when traveling…history, the arts and science are celebrated at many places throughout the land. You'll never know what gems you will find along the way.

Cities, Towns and Waterways: The largest city in the U.S. has over 8 million people. And, there are several towns in the U.S. where your visit can double the population. Traveling around in an RV allows you to explore America's diversity. Visit The Big Apple, the Luggage Capital of the World and the Crossroads of the West. Even though it's too congested to take your RV into big cities, don't avoid them. Stay in a campground on the outskirts, go into the city and take a guided tour to see the city and get an overview of its history and notable features. When traveling from sea to shining sea, give yourself the chance to wade in the Atlantic and Pacific oceans, Lake Michigan, the Gulf of Mexico and the Great Salt Lake…and to cross the Mighty Mississippi many times at multiple locations.

Where To Stay / Park It

Campgrounds and RV parks abound across the country. You see the familiar camping symbol on many interstate exits. In most parts of the country most of the year, campground and RV park sites are available on a drive-in/no reservation basis. However, common sense dictates that in very popular areas or heavily visited places (such as national parks during the summer) reservations are advisable. Snow birds also must plan ahead and make reservations well in advance if they want to ensure a spot for the warm winter season.

The most extensive campground listings can be found in the North American RV Travel Guide, which combines listings from the former Trailer Life and Woodall's directories. There are also a large number of directories and guides available that provide information about private campgrounds, RV parks, resorts, state and federal parks and locations for boondocking (free overnight parking).

The most comprehensive selection of campground guides can be found either at Camping World or in RV bookstores on the Internet. Browse at the bookstores, read the descriptions and ask other RVers which books they use for finding accommodations. There is no one single allinclusive campground directory. You will eventually end up using the two, three or more books most suited to your style, preferences and needs. It's a trial and error process.

How Much Is "Too Much?"

Average daily campground fees can be as low as $25 or as high as $75 depending on your choices. Personal preferences and budget considerations will be key factors when you decide where to stay. Most directories and guides will spell out daily rates and provide at least a general description of the facility.

- Savvy RV travelers quickly learn how to take advantage of the many discounts available to lower overall camping fees:
- Camping clubs can provide discounts from 10% to 50% off daily fees at selected campgrounds.
- Discount coupons can be found in directories and magazines and are distributed at RV shows and rallies.

Some RVers find that boondocking every so often helps to offset escalating campground fees (see the next section in this chapter).

Once you begin traveling, you'll quickly learn about the types of RV parks and campgrounds out there as well as their fees. And you will be able to determine the kinds of campgrounds or RV parks and/or boondocking sites where you're most comfortable. At some point, you may receive a solicitation from a campground membership organization offering a free stay at one of their RV parks or resorts in return for your attendance at a sales presentation. "Campground memberships" are different from "camping clubs." When RVers join a camping club, they are not required to sign a contract and the annual dues are usually small by comparison.

Campground memberships, on the other hand, can include a costly initial fee and requires a contract agreement to pay annual fees. While campground memberships may appear attractive during a sales presentation, it is important to gain sufficient RVing experience before making such a commitment. Some RVers find that campground memberships are suited to their travel schedules and the specific parks in the campground network are attractive enough to justify the investment. But some purchase only to find out later it was not suitable for them.

Money-Saving Programs

Frequent visitors to public lands can get significant savings with the America the Beautiful Senior Pass or Access Pass. These are recreation passes issued by the federal government to provide a discounts on federal use fees for facilities and services such as camping, swimming, parking, boat launching and tours. It does not cover fees charged by concessionaires at federal facilities.

- ***Senior Pass***: This pass is for citizens of the United States who are 62 years of age or older. The cost for a senior pass is $10 and proof of age must be shown. It is a lifetime entrance pass to national parks, monuments, historic sites, recreation areas and national wildlife refuges that charge an entrance fee. The Senior Pass admits the pass signee and any accompanying passengers in a private vehicle.
- ***Access Pass***: This pass is for citizens of the United States who are blind or permanently disabled. The Access Pass is free; proof of medically-determined permanent disability must be shown. It is a lifetime entrance pass to national monuments, historic sites, recreation areas and national wildlife refuges that charge an entrance fee. The passport admits the pass signee and any accompanying passengers in a private vehicle.
- ***Military***: Active duty military and their dependents qualify for a free annual America the Beautiful pass.

Where To Obtain A Pass

The Senior Pass and Access Pass can be obtained in person at a federal recreation site, through an online application form, or through the mail. There is a $10 fee for passes ordered by mail. The annual Military Pass must be obtained in person. Federal recreation areas include the National Park Service, Bureau of Land Management, U.S. Forest Service, U.S. Fish & Wildlife Service and Bureau of Reclamation.

Glossary

- **Adapter** — A device added to the RV power cord that enables the cord to secure a proper fit into a campground electric hookup outlet.
- **Aftermarket** — The part of the RV industry that provides products and services available to RV owners following the initial RV purchase.
- **Age-Restricted Park** — An RV park or resort specifically designated for people who are 55
- and older.
- **Alternator** — An engine-mounted device that produces 12-volt DC electricity for battery charging and other 12-volt functions while the engine is running.
- **Backup Monitoring System** — A rear-mounted camera and a display screen in the cockpit designed to help the driver backing up large vehicles.
- **Big Rig** — A nickname given to the pricey, modern and large (generally with multiple slideouts) Class A motor homes.
- **Black Water** — Waste and water materials generally from the RV's toilet.
- **Black Water Holding Tank** — The tank where the black water is flushed and held until emptied (dumped) later.
- **Blacktop Boondocking** — Free overnight parking without any electric, water or sewer connections in a paved parking area with the property owner's permission. Often called dry camping.
- **Boondocking** — Camping without any electric, water or sewer connections, generally out in the boonies (remote wooded areas) and without paying a camping fee.

- **Break-Away Switch** — A switch that automatically applies the breaks on a vehicle that's being towed should that vehicle break loose from the vehicle that's towing it.
- **Breaking Camp** — All the procedures involved in unhooking and preparing to leave the campsite.
- **Cab** — The cockpit or driver's area of the RV.
- **Camper Van** — A Class B motorized RV.
- **Campground** — An area that has campsites (with hookups) for rent; also has a bath house with showers and toilets.
- **Campsite** — The fee-pay piece of land in a campground that RVs rent. The site generally has electric and water hookups; often – but not always – a sewer hookup is at each site.
- **Campground Host** — A person or couple who is employed by a campground to perform designated duties in return for a rent-free campsite and/or a salary.
- **Caravan** — A group of RVs traveling together, generally with a wagonmaster guide.
- **Central Dump** — A centralized area where an RV can pull up alongside a sewer hookup where black and grey water tanks can be emptied.
- **Class A Motor Home** — A motorized RV built on a specially-designed chassis; can be gas or diesel-powered and provides driving and living areas all in one.
- **Class B Motor Home** — A van camper, typically between 16 and 21 feet, that provides driving and living areas in a single vehicle.
- **Class C Motor Home** — Commonly referred to as the mini-motor home. Built on a van frame, its most distinguishing feature.
- **Clearance** — The distance between a vehicle's exterior height and potential obstructions
- such as bridges and overpasses.
- **Converter** — A device that transforms 120-volt AC into usable 12-volt DC electricity for use on board an RV.
- **COW** — Condo On Wheels. Luxurious big rigs are often called COWs.
- **Diesel Pusher** — A motorhome powered by a rear-mounted diesel engine, equipped to propel rather than pull larger vehicles. Pushers are usually motorhomes over 34 feet in length.
- **Dolly** — A two-wheeled trailer designed to tow a car with either its front wheels or its back
- wheels up off the ground.

- **Dinghy** — An auxiliary vehicle being towed behind a motorized RV.
- **Dry Camping** — Camping without any hookups; usually only done with self-contained RVs.
- **Dump Station** — (See central dump.) An area that has a sewer opening where black and grey water tanks can be emptied.
- **Dump the Tanks** — Procedure of emptying the black and grey water tanks.
- **Electric Hookup** — Connection available at a campsite where the electric cord from the RV is plugged into an outside 120-volt electrical outlet to provide power inside the RV.
- **Engine Power** — 12 volt DC power generated from the RV's or tow vehicle's engine.
- **Fifth Wheel** — Unique type of trailer built to be towed by a pickup truck with a special hitch mounted in the bed of the pickup. It is the largest of the towables.
- **5er** — Nickname for a fifth wheel trailer.
- **Folding Camper Trailer** — Smallest of the towable RVs, it is often called a pop-up. On the road it looks like a small, shallow box; upon arrival at a camp site, it expands up and out to become a tent-type unit on a flat bed.
- **Four-Down Toad** — An auxiliary vehicle being towed behind a motor home with all four wheels down.
- **Fresh Water Hookup** — Connection made from the RV to an outside fresh water source, available at most campsites.
- **Fresh Water Storage Tank** — Tank under the RV where fresh water is stored ready for use.
- **Fresh Water System** — Clean running water system within the RV for all faucets, sinks, shower, water heater and to maintain the water level in the toilet.
- **Full-Timers** — People who live and travel in an RV year-round; sometimes called "365ers."
- **Full Hookup** — A campsite that has water, electric and sewer hookups directly at the site. Often referred to as "3-point" hookup.
- **Generator** — A device driven by an internal combustion engine that produces 120-volt electricity to be used in the RV when other sources of electricity are not available.
- **Gooseneck** — The part of the fifth wheel trailer that fits into the bed of the pickup truck to

- make a connection for towing.
- **Grey Water** — Used water from the RV sinks, tub and shower.
- **Grey Water Holding Tank** — Tanks where the grey water is held until it is emptied (dumped).
- **Gross Combined Vehicle Weight Rating (GCVW)** — The maximum weight limit for a tow vehicle, object or vehicle being towed and all passengers, cargo and liquid inside.
- **Hitch** — The device that provides a connection between the tow vehicle and the vehicle being towed. There are various classes of hitches depending on the weight they are designed to pull.
- **Hookups** — Outside utilities that are made available for an RV to use; these include electric,
- water, sewer, cable TV and phone.
- **Jacks** — Stabilizing apparatus that are manually or electronically lowered to level and stabilize an RV after it is parked at its campsite.
- **Kingpin** — The part of a fifth wheel trailer that slides and locks into the hitch that is mounted in the bed of the pickup truck tow vehicle.
- **Leveling Bar** — Part of the hitch designed to properly disperse the weight among the axles.
- **LP Gas** — Propane that fuels many of the appliances on board the RV.
- **Making Camp** — All the procedures involved in pulling in, hooking up and preparing for a
- stay at the campsite.
- **Mini-Motor Home** — See Class C Motor Home.
- **Monitor Panel** — A display unit inside the RV that provides information about the on board systems including levels of the tanks and voltage being used in the electrical system.
- **Motor Home** — See Class A Motor Home.
- **No-Toad** — Nickname for the Class B van campers because they generally do not tow a
- dinghy.
- **Pop-Up** — Smallest of the towable RVs, also called a Folding Camper Trailer. On the road it looks like a small, shallow box; upon arrival at a camp site, it expands up and out to become a tent-type unit on a flat bed.

- **Propane** — See LP gas.
- **Pull-Through Site** — A campsite with access from either end, allowing the RV to pull directly into the site, thus eliminating the need to back into the site.
- **Pusher** — See diesel pusher.
- **Rally** — A large get-together of RVers, often sponsored by a camping club or organization.
- **Recreational Vehicle (RV)** — A home-on-wheels that provides the convenience of travel and living quarters all in the same vehicle.
- **Rig** — A nickname used to refer to the entire RV unit, either tow vehicle and trailer or motor home and toad.
- **RV Dinosaur** — Nickname for RVs that are more than 20 years old.
- **RV Newbies** — People who are new to the RV lifestyle.
- **RV Park** — A campground that is more modern, generally featuring longer, wider sites to accommodate newer rigs.
- **RV Resort** — An RV park with larger sites and amenities such as pool, spa, golf, tennis, etc.
- **RV Show** — A venue for displaying the latest recreational vehicles and products and in the
- same location.
- **RV Wannabies** — People who have never gone RVing but who are planning to become
- RVers in the future.
- **Safety Chains** — Additional towing attachment that prevents a towed vehicle from veering off in case of separation during transit.
- **Sewer Connection** — Connection at a campsite that allows the black and grey water tanks
- to be emptied right at the site.
- **Site** — Short for campsite.
- **Slideout** — Sections of the RV's interior that expand outward several feet after the RV is parked. The slideouts widen the inside rooms and create more space on board.
- **Snow Bird** — RVers who spend the winter season in warmer climates and return north during warm weather months.

- **Snow Bird Park** — RV park or resort that caters to retirees who spend the winter season in
- sun-belt states.
- **Sport Utility Trailer** — Sometimes called "toy haulers," this specially designed trailer has living quarters plus a garage at the back to store cycles, ATVs and other sports vehicles or equipment.
- **Stick-Built House** — Any house or home not on wheels; a site-built home.
- **Surge Protector** — A device attached between an incoming electrical power source and the RV designed to intercept any power surges or spikes that could harm RV wiring and appliances.
- **Sway Control Bar** — An accessory device designed to stabilize and restrict motion between a tow vehicle and the vehicle being towed.
- **Toad** — A dinghy or auxiliary vehicle being towed behind a motor home.
- **Tow Bar** — A device used for towing a dinghy behind a motor home.
- **Tow Rating** — The maximum weight a vehicle can safely tow.
- **Tow Vehicle** — The vehicle responsible for towing another vehicle.
- **Towable** — An RV that relies on another vehicle to tow it.
- **Travel Trailer** — The most common towable RV. Its sub-class is a lightweight travel trailer.
- **Truck Camper** — A camper attached to the bed of a pickup truck.
- **Van Camper** — See Class B Motor Home.
- **Walk-Around** — Final check of the RV prior to leaving a campsite or boondocking spot. Walk-around routine includes checking the interior and exterior of the vehicle(s) and check of the surrounding area.
- **Water Pump** — Device designed to force water from the fresh water tank through the pipes
- on board the RV.
- **Wagonmaster** — An individual who is responsible for leading an RV caravan.
- **Workamper** — A general term that refers to people who work at campgrounds as well as campers/travelers who work during the course of their travels.

www.ingramcontent.com/pod-product-compliance
Lightning Source LLC
Chambersburg PA
CBHW081617100526

44590CB00021B/3476